Ellsworth M. Kisner
1943.

CONQUEST OF THE SOUTHERN PLAINS

Uncensored Narrative of the Battle of the Washita
and Custer's Southern Campaign

Golden Saga Series

By CHARLES J. BRILL

Author of

"What Indian Tongues Could Tell"

"Dog Soldier"

"Red Knights"

"Before '89"

GOLDEN SAGA PUBLISHERS
Oklahoma City

To the memory of Frank Rush, plainsman, friend of the Indian, this narrative is gratefully dedicated. His lifelong friendship for his red brother and his sympathetic efforts to lighten the later-day load of the Red Knights of the Southern Plains unsealed rebellious lips and brought forth many essential facts which heretofore have been kept secret by those who opposed Custer's ruthless conquest of the Washita.

BATTLE OF THE WASHITA

Reproduced from General Custer's "Wild Life on the Plains."

"Contact of civilization with barbarism is the scandal of history."

WENDELL PHILLIPS

TABLE OF CONTENTS

ILLUSTRATIONS

"I never knew an Indian chief to break his word. * * * I have lived on this frontier fifty years and I have never yet known an instance in which war broke out with these tribes that the tribes were not in the right."

GENERAL WILLIAM S. HARNEY

INTRODUCTION

Wanted~Jobs for Generals

*T*HEY still are writing about the Battle of the Little Big Horn; of that dramatic finale to the ten-year campaign General George A. Custer waged against nomadic legions of the Western Plains from what is now Oklahoma to Montana; of that tragic June encounter when Custer and more than two hundred fifty of those who followed him in that ill-advised charge against the Sioux and their allies met the same fate they had meted out to so many of their bronzed enemies in the southern sector.

There seems to be a tendency to accept the so-called "Custer Massacre" on the Little Big Horn as the pivotal engagement of the white man's conquest of the prairies. Perhaps, in a way it is entitled to that distinction; yet, as a "decisive battle" it does not compare with the Battle of the Washita, waged in what is now Western Oklahoma, eight years previously. Too, the Battle of the Washita had an indirect bearing on Custer's debacle in Montana.

Both of these historic encounters were anomalies. In each instance it must be recorded that Custer was repulsed. He retreated under cover of darkness after sacking only the smallest of several villages on the Washita he had set out to conquer. His entire detachment was annihilated on the Little Big Horn. Still, the after effects of these two Indian victories of arms played a more important part in subjugating the Plains tribes than all other engagements combined.

Custer blazed a crimson trail from one end of the Plains to the other. He was merciless to man and beast. He was ruthless in treatment of his foes. An Indian was an Indian to him; and it is a matter of record that he killed more Indian women and children than warriors. That he never was successful in capturing an Indian warrior in battle can be substantiated. His sole prisoners of war were decrepit old men, squaws and papooses. Not once, during his ten years' crusade, did he ever defeat in battle the red knights who opposed him.'

Never before has anyone attempted to carry his reader from one end of this trail to the other, assigning to each incident its relative importance. Such is the purpose of this narrative. It will strive to establish the eventual significance of many incidents which, were they considered individually, would seem trivial and entirely lacking in major consequence. Properly correlated, however, they are epochal.

1. Custer failed to contact, personally, the Indians for a single engagement during his first border campaign, that of 1867, commonly known as the Hancock Expedition. This cost the government $9,000,000 and claimed the lives of more than three hundred whites, settlers, teamsters and soldiers, while only four warriors were killed.

His next opportunity occurred in the early autumn of 1868. The very day he rejoined the Seventh Cavalry on Bluff Creek, Southwestern Kansas, after lifting of his court-martial sentence, Indians made a series of running attacks on his camp. Though hundreds of shots were fired, not an Indian was killed. Eventually the assailants rode tauntingly away, passing in full view within a few hundred yards of Custer and his men as they departed. Despite the fact that he had seven hundred soldiers with him at the time, outnumbering the Indians several to one, Custer did not give chase. ("Life on the Plains," page 171).

In his own memoirs ("Life on the Plains," page 222) Custer admits he retreated from the so-called Battle of the Washita during the night of November 27, 1868, as a result of the press of warriors on all sides.

His next clash with the Indians was during the Yellowstone Expedition of 1873. Here Sioux attacked his command of some four-score soldiers. Custer was rescued by the timely arrival of reinforcements, but for which he might have suffered the same fate as overtook him on the Little Big Horn three years later, when his entire command was annihilated. (Whitaker's "Life of Custer," page 495.)

The Little Big Horn battle was his only other fight with Plains Indians.

WANTED—JOBS FOR GENERALS

Indian conflicts during that period immediately following the Civil War, with which this narrative will deal, might well be ascribed, in a great measure, to "generals without jobs." Close of the struggle between states dropped many West Pointers from the breveted rank of general to that of colonel, major, even captain. It also left many aspiring military leaders with personal ambitions ungratified. Conquest of the Plains offered the only avenue for action which would restore rank and yield glory.

One such was Custer. A major general by brevet at the termination of the Civil War, he immediately was reduced to the rank of captain and assigned to routine duty in Texas.

Indian wars, deliberately fomented, restored his generalship and made him the greatest popular hero of that period. These wars form the subject of this narrative, a story controverting versions heretofore accepted as authentic.

Discrepancies between this story and former popular written recitals of the same events are not difficult to explain. Virtually everything the world has read of the happenings of that memorable encounter on the Washita and contemporaneous events has been gleaned from Custer's own official reports now in the archives of the War Department in Washington, or from Custer's own published memoirs. Only in recent years has there begun to dawn a conviction that these memoirs are woefully deficient in vital details; that there are statements contained therein which might be proved contrary to actual facts.

For instance, one may search Custer's reports and his memoirs in vain to discover how gallant Major Elliott and his equally gallant followers came to be cut off from the main body of troops and just how they met their deaths on the Washita. One may search in vain for details of the assassination of Black Kettle, head chief of the Cheyennes, slain as Custer dashed into his peaceful village. One cannot read in Custer's writings of the actual motives which caused Custer to beat such a hasty retreat under cover of darkness without ascertaining the fate of his missing cavalrymen. Nor can one justify Custer's boast in his official report that he had killed more than one hundred warriors in that one engagement, when, as a matter of fact, during all his service on the Southern Plains, Custer and his men accounted for less than a score of braves, most of his victims, killed, wounded and prisoners, being squaws and children.[2]

Not once does the name of Ben Clark appear in all of Custer's voluminous writings in connection with his Wichita campaign; yet Clark was his chief of scouts. It was Clark's firm protest against attacking the other villages on the Washita which unquestionably prevented annihilation of the Seventh Cavalry on that occasion. Custer, in a delirium of victory, would have swept on down the valley despite knowledge that ammunition of his command was practically exhausted and that thousands of warriors, thirsting for revenge, swarmed that vicinity. General Sheridan, Custer's superior, pronounced Ben Clark the greatest scout he ever had known. It was Clark's masterful guidance of Custer's men during the Washita campaign which prompted this pronouncement.[3]

Conspicuous to all those who know the full story

2. Magpie and Little Beaver named twelve Indian braves killed during Custer's attack on Black Kettle's village. They said they were positive not more than two or three other warriors were killed at that time. Both asserted that several times that many women and children were slain. Report of the Secretary of Interior, 1869-70, page 525, says thirteen men, sixteen women and nine children. Sheridan's official report, quoting Custer's figures, boasts "one hundred three warriors killed." ("Life on the Plains," page 238.)

of the Washita is ommission of the name of Quar-
master James Bell and all but superficial, incidental
mention of his daring dash to deliver ammunition
to Custer's men at a time when the Indians were
pressing hard and the troopers had practically exhausted their supply of cartridges. Custer virtually
ignored the incident in his account of the battle,
yet, in recognition of this exploit, a resolution was
introduced in Congress years afterward to award
Quartermaster Bell the Congressional Medal   of
Honor. In honor of him, one of the tributaries of
the Washita not far from the battlefield, is named
"Quartermaster Creek."

Custer rode to his death at the opposite extremity of the far-flung trouble zone several years later
without supplying missing details or correcting his
erroneous official reports. Those who swooped down
on Black Kettle's unsuspecting camp in the gray of
dawn also are gone. So, too, are nearly all of those
who bore the brunt of this unwarranted attack; who
put Custer on the spot out on the plains of Texas;
who dogged his footsteps until they had avenged all
wrongs, real or fancied, in the rugged fastnesses
of Montana; those who gave him the soubriquet of

3. How Ben Clark out-talked Custer and prevailed upon
him to abandon the idea of attacking the other villages was
told to Claude E. Hensley by Romero, who was present
when this incident occurred. Romero told Mr. Hensley that
all the other scouts concurred in Clark's opinion. In his
own memoirs, however, Custer takes full credit for orig-
inating this piece of strategy. The writer obtained this
information personally from Mr. Hensley.

Custer always resented this interference   by   Clark.
Some two weeks later, Clark again incurred Custer's animosity. This time the second expedition had reached Whet-
stone Creek, east of the Washita battlefield. The banks
were so precipitous the wagons could not cross at that point.
Custer proposed a twenty-five mile detour. Clark said the
stream could be crossed near the point where it emptied
into the Washita. Custer insisted this was not so. General Sheridan, who was in command, took Clark's advice and
found it to be sound. These two incidents Clark blamed for
Custer's failure to mention his name in any of his writings.

"Creeping Panther," "Yellow Hair," and "Strong Arm."

Custer and his contemporaries treated those who contested possession of the Plains with the white men as barbarians. Plains Indians reverse this designation. They consider Custer the actual barbarian of that crusade.

Let each reader judge this for himself.

Those to whom this information was entrusted by Indian survivors were honor bound not to divulge it in its revolting entirety so long as the brave little woman who shared many of the vicissitudes of frontier life with her illustrious husband should live.

This vow of mutual silence was a fitting tribute to the woman who idolized the fiery young cavalry leader from girlhood until they parted as Custer began that last long trek to the land of the Sioux, from which he never returned. It was acknowledgment of the fortitude she displayed while accompanying him into the land of the wild, marauding Indians, there to wait stout-heartedly for his return from a dash deep into the enemy's country, cheering him meanwhile by letters borne through many dangers by intrepid couriers; or to ride madly with him in the chase after buffalo; or to grace his side at the gay, though necessarily crude, social events of frontier army posts by which they whiled away intervals between expeditions. Those who made this pact did not desire to cast a shadow over the spirits of this widow as she rode alone down her sunset trail.

So long did she survive, however, that most of those cognizant of the story to be told preceded her into the beyond. Magpie, venerable Cheyenne chieftain, entered the happy hunting grounds two years before Mrs. Custer. Left Hand, wrinkled Arapahoe warrior, followed Magpie a few months later. Little Beaver, another grizzled Cheyenne survivor of the Washita, joined them soon thereafter. Frank Rush, pioneer plainsman, whose efforts in behalf of the so-called "wild" Plains tribesmen, unsealed lips that had been tightly closed for more than three score years, also has gone to his last rest. He lies near the spot where General Sheridan established headquarters at the eastern edge of the Wichitas while Custer pursued the last of the Kiowas, Cheyennes and Arapahoes into the desert wastes to the west. Of the original group who pieced together this story there are left only John Otterby, noted scout and Cheyenne interpreter, and the writer. It is up to me to tell the story.

If, in its recitation, the courage of Custer seems questioned, let it be remembered that Sheridan reprimanded him for quitting the Washita without ascertaining the fate of Major Elliott and his missing detachment. Let it be known, too, that descendants of those red riders who swarmed ridges on either side of the Washita that bleak November evening challenge to this day: "Why didn't Custer stay and fight? Why did he run away in the night, taking with him as prisoners only squaws and papooses? Why did he falsify in his official report regarding what happened there that day?"

It is difficult, very difficult, to challenge the courage of a man who captured the first colors taken by the Army of the Potomac; who served with McDowell at Bull Run; who foiled Stuart at Gettysburg; who was accorded the honor of receiving the flag of truce upon surrender of Lee at Appomattox.

If Custer seemingly is charged with perfidy in breaking his plighted word to the Indians when they had him and his command at their mercy on the Staked Plains of Texas a few months later, let it be remembered Custer paid in full for any such breach of faith on the Little Big Horn just seven years afterward.

CONQUEST OF THE SOUTHERN PLAINS

This story is told, not to discredit Custer, but to give credit where credit is due, to throw discerning light upon the stirring events incident to the Indian wars of the late 'Sixties and early 'Seventies. It is told that the world might have the Indian's side of the white man's ruthless conquest of the prairies to lay alongside the white man's story for individual conjecture. It is told that the mystery surrounding the fatal sortie of the "troopers Custer forgot" be solved at last.

Facts contained herein have been gleaned from a multitude of reliable sources.

Most of the heart throbs in the story of the Battle of the Washita were contributed by aged Indians who, then boys in their 'teens, were among members of Black Kettle's village who managed to escape when Custer's Seventh Cavalry made its engulfing charge. To Chief Magpie, a distant relative of Black Kettle, we are indebted for the only eye-witness story of the assassination of that great Cheyenne leader. From Magpie and Little Beaver, another member of Black Kettle's village, and from Left Hand, an Arapahoe in one of the lower encampments, comes the only authentic story of how Elliot came to be separated from Custer's main command, how his retreat was cut off and how he and his entire following met the fate that was inevitable when Custer failed to come to their rescue.

None of these informants could speak English. Their story was related through the interpretations of John Otterby, last of the famous scouts, interpreters and mediaries who served the Government during the stirring days immediately after conclusion of major hostilities on the Southern Plains. That their recollections might be more vivid and their disclosures accurate, they were taken by the writer, on more than one occasion, to the historic battlefield. There their revelations were made.

From Chief Magpie were obtained countless disclosures of heretofore unchronicled incidents connected with major events—the Sand Creek Massacre of 1864 from which Black Kettle miraculously escaped; the Washita Battle in which Black Kettle was killed and Magpie was wounded; how the Cheyennes applied the Sacred Arrow ceremony to Custer on the Sweetwater; happenings at the Battle of the Little Big Horn, whither Magpie had accompanied a band of Cheyennes which had followed Custer for seven years to avenge the Sacred Arrows and their martyred contemporaries.

Magpie's contributions to this narrative do not represent heresay evidence. They are the faithful recitals of things he saw with his own eyes, incidents in which he was an actual participant. He and his father were the first from the outside to reach the Sand Creek shambles after Colonel Chivington and his butchers had departed. So far as is known, he is the only person who saw Black Kettle mount his horse and receive his death wounds as Custer led the charge on the Washita village. It is not difficult to account for this fortunate circumstance. It will be apparent when the reader reaches that part of this story.

Magpie was one of those young braves who watched Custer approach Medicine Arrow's village on the Sweetwater, who loitered without as the Cheyenne elders put the white soldier chief through the arrow ceremony that March afternoon and who, from the back of his pony, high up on the ridge between Custer's camp and that of the Indians, witnessed Custer's futile efforts to seize all of the principal chiefs to be held as hostages.

It was Magpie's disclosures in regard to the arrow ceremony referred to above which enabled the writer to fathom the significance of this unprecedented event, a significance which never before has been placed upon what Custer lightly referred to in his memoirs as a humorous, trivial incident. So far as is known to any living person, this is the only time such use ever was made of the shafts so sacred to the Cheyennes.

In only one instance did Magpie deviate from his firm stand against hearsay evidence. This was in the matter of the mistreatment of the women prisoners Custer carried away from the Washita. When hard pressed for comment on this subject, Magpie said he had heard some of the victims recount experiences corroborating the story of indignities Little Beaver said his mother, Red Dress, one of these prisoners, told upon her return to her people.

Red Dress was no inconsequential personage among the women of the Cheyenne nation. It was she who ministered to the needs of a Cheyenne woman who gave birth to a baby girl in the sand pits on Sand Creek while the terrible struggle raged between desperate defenders of these improvised breastworks and Chivington's blood-mad troopers. It was she who appealed to Romeo, one of Custer's half-breed interpreter-scouts, to save the women and children of Black Kettle's camp from anticipated atrocities after their surrender. Out of gratitude for this intervention, Red Dress later offered Romeo one of her daughters to be his wife.

It was Red Dress who related how, when the troops had returned to Camp Supply with the women prisoners taken on the Washita, Custer and his officers approached the cowering group to select companions for a convivial night. Her story of this occurance has been corroborated by Big Horse, a Cheyenne chief whose wife was one of those subjected to these indignities.

In some respects Magpie's account of the killing and burial of Black Kettle differed so far from

COMMEMORATING WASHITA BATTLE

This photograph was made by the writer on the Washita Battlefield, on the occasion of the sixty-second anniversary of that engagement. Left to right: John Otterby, interpreter; Magpie; Little Beaver; Left Hand, who furnished many of the details of that massacre. Magpie, Little Beaver and Left Hand were participants in this encounter.

popular version of these incidents that at first some were inclined to doubt his entire story. Four years of checking and re-checking have confounded his critics and have confirmed Magpie's version which he so staunchly defended. In contrast to Magpie's authentic description of Black Kettle's slaying, Trotter, a young Osage member of Custer's Indian scouts, boasted that he had singled out Black Kettle during the fighting in the village and, in desperate hand-to-hand battle, had dispatched the Cheyenne chief. He claimed to have then lifted Black Kettle's scalp.

More recently, a Cheyenne still living, who professes to be a descendant of this noted chieftain, related that Black Kettle's body was not recovered by his people until several days after the battle; that it had been partly devoured by wolves; that the remains, upon being recovered, were "buried" in the forks of a tree.

Magpie said he helped recover Black Kettle's body the day after the massacre; that it was lying in the Washita, entirely submerged except the face; that it had not been scalped. He said he helped the women carry it up the bank, out along the pony trail a considerable distance and then, turning from the trail, deposit it upon a sandy knoll. At the time he took his departure the women were debating whether they should bury it there or still father away on higher ground.

These disputed points would be of little moment were it not that later events confirmed Magpie's account, thereby strengthening confidence in other portions of his remarkable story.

This confirmation came July 13, 1934. While workmen were excavating for a bridge fill at the western edge of the battlefield, they unearthed a skeleton. Ornaments and trinkets found with the skeleton were identified as similar to those worn and possessed by Black Kettle. It was found near the exact spot where Magpie had said he helped deposit Black Kettle's body. Certain conditions of the remains, as described by those who accidentally discovered it, preclude the possibility that wolves had desecrated it. The fact that it was found under five feet of earth discounted the report of another that the body had been accorded a tree burial.

Especial recognition is due the valuable services of John Otterby, interpreter. His assistance was required repeatedly for interrogation of those venerable Indians whose disclosures made available much of the most valuable information contained herein.

John Otterby is the son of Charles Autobee, a French-Canadian who served as scout for soldiers at Fort Laramine, Wyoming, and a Cheyenne woman he married there. Coming to the Southern Plains as a mere boy, Otterby scouted and served as messenger for a band of white renegades operating from the Palo Duro Canyon in the Texas panhandle. Later, he joined the Government service as a member of General Miles' company of Indian police stationed at Fort Reno shortly after that fort was established near the Darlington Cheyenne-Arapahoe Indian agency. He frequently served as interpreter for General Miles in some of his most important conferences with these Indians, for General Sheridan and for many other government agents prior to opening of Indian Territory to white settlement. He put in nearly a score of years in the Government's service as scout and interpreter.

Today John Otterby ranks high among the leading men of the Cheyenne tribe. He is a member of the Cheyenne-Arapahoe tribal council.

Gratitude also is expressed to Kish Hawkins, interpreter for the Cheyenne-Arapahoe agency at Concho, Oklahoma. Hawkins is a grandson of White

Antelope, noted Cheyenne chief slain during the Sand Creek massacre of 1864.

Acknowledgment of assistance rendered by many others in assembling and verifying salient facts further is made. Particularly valuable has been that of Claude E. Hensley, who, as a young newspaperman in El Reno, as early as 1892 earned the confidence and friendship of many of those white scouts who accompanied the Washita Expedition. These included Ben Clark, Edmund Guerrier, John Poisell, Jesse Stewart Morrison, Romero and Jack Stilwell. Mr. Hensley associated with these men for years. Through this intimate association, he learned a wealth of unpublished information which he generously has contributed to this narrative. His collection of frontier photographs has furnished some of the illustrations contained herein.

Lastly, simply because his was the final contribution, appreciation is expressed to Dr. J. B. Thoburn, formerly curator of the Oklahoma State Historical Society, and, at this writing, a member of the board of directors of that organization, for his courtesy in reviewing this completed manuscript, and for certain factual information contained in the text.

Included in the scores of books and documents which provided pertinent data may be listed:

General George A. Custer's "Life on the Plains," 1874.

General Philip Sheridan's "Personal Recollections," 1888.

Elizabeth Bacon Custer's "Following the Guidon," 1890, and the same author's "Boots and Saddles."

General Richard Irving Dodge's "Our Wild Indians," 1881.

David L. Spott's "Campaigning with Custer," 1926.

Captain Frederick Whittaker's "Popular Life of General George A. Custer," 1876.

D. B. Randolph Keim's "Sheridan's Troopers," 1870.

Captain W. S. Nye's "Carbine and Lance," 1937.

George Bird Grinnell's "The Fighting Cheyennes," 1915.

Colonel Henry Inman's "Tales of the Trail," 1898.

Olive Dixon's "Life and Adventures of Billy Dixon," as revised by Dr. J. B. Thoburn.

E. A. Brininstool's "Fighting Red Cloud's Warriors," 1926.

Colonel W. A. Graham's "Custer's Last Fight," 1926.

Lewis F. Crawford's "Rekindling Campfires," 1926.

W. Fletcher Johnson's "Life of Sitting Bull and History of Indian Wars," 1890.

Government Documents, "Conditions of American Indians," 1867.

Annual Reports Commissioner of Indian Affairs, 1860-1890.

Various other official documents and publications of the United States Government.

Oklahoma Redbook, 1912.

In building a comprehensive background of knowledge of the traits, manners, customs, beliefs and conditions of Plains Indians, invaluable information was gleaned from:

George Catlin's "Letters and Notes of the Manners, Customs, and Conditions of the North American Indians," 1859.

Captain Randolph B. Marcy's "Exploration of Red River," and the same author's "Thirty Years of Army Life on the Border," both published in 1854.

Captain W. H. Milburn's "Lance, Cross and Canoe," 1892.

C. B. Walker's "The Mississippi Valley," 1880.

J. H. Beadle's "Five Years in the Territories," 1873.

Washington Irving's "Tour of the Prairies."

Frank A. Root's "The Overland Stage to California," 1901.

Francis Parkman's "Oregon Trail," 1846.

Mitchell's School Geography and Atlas, 1852.

Oklahoma State Historical Society's "Chronicles of Oklahoma."

CHAPTER ONE

George Armstrong Custer

$\mathcal{G}$EORGE Armstrong Custer was a born soldier. Military blood had filled the veins of the Custers as far back as there is any record of the family. This carries back slightly more than a century prior to General Custer's death on the Little Big Horn. It starts with the great grandfather of the man who led the Seventh U. S. Cavalry during a decade of campaigning on the Western frontier. That great grandfather, Kuster by name, came to America as a Hessian officers serving the British during the American Revolution.

When Burgoyne surrendered, Kuster was one of the paroled Hessians who took up his abode in the new country. All of the direct descendants of Kuster from that time on wore a uniform and carried arms. George Custer's father, Emmanuel, was a member of the Ohio State Militia. It was during this service of his father that George obtained his first military uniform. Though he was only four years old at the time, no commander-in-chief ever wore his trappings with greater pride than that which swelled young Custer's breast as this tow-headed youngster would don the uniform his mother had made for him and attempt to drill at the heels of his father's company. With a wooden gun he learned the manual of arms during this early "enlistment."

Custer's birthplace was Harrison County, Ohio; the date December 5, 1839. His earliest boyhood was spent on the farm. When only ten years old "Autie," as he was called, accompanied his sister to Monroe, Michigan, where he was to become a pupil in Stebbins' Academy. Here, too, he was thrilled with the knowledge that he was treading a region made sacred by the blood of eight hundred mounted Kentucky riflemen annihilated by the British general, Proctor, supported by the famous Shawnee chief, Tecumseh, thirty-six years previously. Perhaps stories of this Frenchtown debacle may have had a direct or indirect bearing on his vicious attitude toward the Plains Indians with whom he was destined to clash so often during the closing years of his life.

His academic days also brought Custer into contact with the girl who later was to become his wife and accompany him during his peace-time residence on the Plains. She was Elizabeth Bacon, daughter of Monroe's first citizen, Judge Daniel S. Bacon.

Their first companionship, however, soon was to be broken. Custer went back to Ohio to teach school and to seek ways and means of attaining his ambition to enter West Point. At the age of seventeen he obtained this appointment.

Like every other period of Custer's life, that at the United States Military Academy was filled by stirring events. It included his first court-martial. This came during the closing months of his Academy career when, as officer of the guard, he urged on a fist fight between cadets instead of stopping it. It came near preventing his graduation with his class.

Since Custer craved action, he was not long to be denied the thing he always desired. Civil war was already breaking in full force at the time he received his lieutenant's commission in mid-summer 1861. Delaying only long enough to equip himself with uniform, sabre, revolver, sash and spurs, he hastened to Washington to report for service.

It is a matter of record that Custer got many lucky breaks, as many as ever came to any man in military service. Here came one of them. The day he reported for service he was presented to General Winfield Scott, Commander-in-Chief of the Union armies. Within half an hour he had been assigned to bear dispatches from General Scott to General McDowell commanding the principal army in the field. McDowell then was about to clash with General Beauregard's Confederates. By sundown Custer was on his way. Within another twenty-four hours he had engaged in his first battle—the Second Battle of Bull Run, a defeat for the forces he so recently had joined.

More lucky breaks came rapidly for the young officer. Upon re-organization of the Federal forces, Custer found himeslf under General Philip Kearny. Almost immediately he was made aide-de-camp to that officer. Shortly afterward he was advanced to adjutant general.

Service under this strict disciplinarian appears to have influenced Custer's later conduct when he became a commander of troops against the Indians. Custer's comments on Kearny's characteristics might well have been applied to the young cavalryman's own demeanor several years later. Of Kearny Custer wrote:

"Kearny was a man of violent passions, quick and determined impulses, haughty demeanor. . . brave as the bravest of men can be, possessed of unusually great activity, both mental and physical, patriotic as well as ambitious, impatient under all delay. . . He constantly chafed under the restraint and inactivity of camp life and never was so happy and contented as when moving to the attack. . . Brave in battle, impetuous in command, and at times domineering toward those beneath him, no one could wear a more courtly manner than Kearny unless he willed to do otherwise."

In this description one can substitute the name

of "Custer" for "Kearny" and have a true picture.

Custer's early service was with the Second Cavalry. Transferred to the Fifth when he joined the Army of the Potomac in 1862, he led his first charge at Cedar Run. His captain and senior lieutenant being absent, Custer was given the honor of directing a company ordered to drive back the enemy's pickets. During this skirmish one of his men was shot through the head, first casualty for the Army of the Potomac.

Throughout his Civil War service Custer was brought into contact repeatedly with those who were to have a bearing on his Plains service. He was serving under General Hancock in the Williamsburg campaign and it was to be under this same commander that he received his introduction to Indian warfare. General George B. McClellan was commander-in-chief of the Army of the Potomac. This was the same McClellan who, as a young engineer, had made the first survey of the north fork of Red River past the Wichita Mountains and on to the Staked Plains of Texas with the Marcy expedition of 1853. Custer was to invade that same region and to follow part of McClellan's trail in pursuit of Cheyennes, Araphoes and Kiowas, nearly sixteen years later. It was McClelland who, discovering the value of Lieutenant Custer as a scout, obtained his promotion to rank of captain and his attachment to headquarter's staff.

Custer's first service in his new capacity was to lead a daylight attack on an enemy picket post during the Chickahominy campaign. He killed many, took others prisoners and captured the first Confederate color taken by the Army of the Potomac.

Followed defeat of McClellan in the Seven Days' Battle and McClellan's removal from command. Into temporary retirement Custer followed his chief, only to be returned to active service

GENERAL GEORGE A. CUSTER

in time to distinguish himself in a cavalry engagement at the Battle of Aldie. This performance elevated him to the rank of brigadier general. Then came his assignment to command the afterward famous Michigan brigade.

Gettysburg, Rapidan, and other engagements saw Custer in brilliant action. Then came his marriage to Miss Bacon and his return to service in the Wilderness campaign. At Winchester he served under General Phil Sheridan for the first time. Sheridan later was to be his co-leader in the campaign against Indians along the Washita. At Winchester, Custer's brigade served with distinction. After Winchester was won Custer was made a division commander under General Averill. His crushing victory of Woodstock Races became an epic of the war, followed soon thereafter by that at Cedar Creek. Eventually came the climax at Appomattox when Custer received from General Lee the flag of truce that meant the close of the war between the states.

For some, however, the war was not over. Far out in Texas there was a large Confederate army under Kirby Smith toward which Jefferson Davis was making his way when intercepted and captured. This army was not engaged in open hostilities at the time but its presence presented the possibility of a rebellion which might take Texas out of the Union and make it and independent state once more. Thither General Sheridan was sent and Custer was ordered to follow. Though danger of a successful secession of Texas soon passed, there remained the menace of guerilla warfare to cope with. To cope with it Custer was believed to be eminently fitted. For that reason he was permitted to continue to his destination even though Smith's surrender came before the young officer had arrived at New Orleans on his way to the far southwestern front.

When Custer was mustered out of the volunteer service in Texas, early in 1866, he was reduced to rank of captain. Immediately he received an offer from President Juarez of Mexico to take command of his cavalry forces in his second war against the interloper, Maximilian. The offer of handsome pay and an opportunity for the active service he loved appealed to Custer. But he had to obtain permission of the president of the United States before he could accept. It so happened that Andrew Johnson, who had become president upon the assassination of Abraham Lincoln, had other plans for this famous young officer. Afraid he, too, might become the victim of an assassin's bullet, Johnson wanted a competent body-guard as he traveled through the States. Who could serve better than Custer? He chose Custer, and the opportunity for foreign fighting had passed.

Reorganization of the Seventh Cavalry that autumn for duty on the Western frontier was a welcome event, so far as Custer was concerned. It brought him the rank of lieutenant-colonel and prospect, not only of increased pay and the thrill of Indian fighting, but of buffalo hunting as well. During his stay in Texas Custer had a taste of big game hunting. He had acquired a pack of wolf hounds. Duty on the Plains would give him an opportunity to hunt to his heart's content, so he thought, even while engaged in the more hazardous task of warring on Plains Indians. He did take his favorite dogs with him to Kansas, and even while on the scout for Indians, frequently hunted buffalo with his wolfhounds.

His peculiar temperament brought many sudden, contrasting and even contradictory transformations throughout Custer's life. As a boy he had been mischievous, but never bad, never sullen, never sulking. He was tender hearted, his biographers insisting he could not even stand to see a fowl beheaded for the table. As a youth he was of kindly disposition. He possessed tireless energy and always was up to pranks, even during his West Point days. There he underwent a change of character, developing jealousies and engendering enmities which were continued throughout the remainder of his life.

Included in these enmities was one with Lieutenant William Babcock Hazen. Lieutenant Hazen chanced to be officer of the day at West Point that eventful day when Custer, as officer of the guard, urged on a fist fight between cadets instead of separating them as he should have done under the regulations. Happening that way while the fight was in process, Lieutenant Hazen accosted Custer and asked him why he had encouraged this breach of rules. Hazen was forced by the regulations to place Custer under arrest and to appear against him before the court martial. For this Custer never forgave Hazen, carrying animosity in his heart toward this fellow officer to the day of his death.

By a coincidence, one of those which continually were occurring throughout Custer's life, this same Hazen was stationed at Fort Cobb as agent of all Southern Plains tribes at the time Custer made his invasion of the Washita. Despite Hazen's efforts to prevent Custer's molestation of the tribes under his jurisdiction, which the agent insisted were not hostiles, Custer rode ruthlessly on. Subsequently, it was Hazen's representations in matters pertaining to the Black Kettle massacre and pursuit of the other Washita villages which brought public condemnation down upon the head of Custer for his evident persecution of these Indians.

Himself studiously disregarding many of the established army regulations during service in the Civil War, Custer later became a harsh taskmaster, a "man of violent passions, quick and determined impulses, haughty demeanor, impetuous in command and at times domineering toward those beneath him." He became a severe disciplinarian. During his brief command in Texas he resorted to flogging and to head shaving as disciplinarian measures. His attitude toward his men caused him to be thoroughly hated by all under him. This in violent contrast to the idolatry which his men had accorded him during his brilliant leadership a year or so previously.

Then there were two striking incidents of a similar nature during the Washita campaign. On the morning set for start of the first expedition south of the Cimarron, some of the officers were slow about getting under way. Entering a tent where his brother, Captain Tom Custer, was eating breakfast, the general kicked the victual-laden table clear across the tent as he harshly ordered his brother to "fall in," breakfastless, for a hard march in deep snow and bitter cold.

A few weeks later while the expedition was camped at Fort Cobb, some of the civilian teamsters, growing tired of their daily fare of wild game, decided to buy a yearling beef for Christmas dinner. Johnny Murphy, a boy driver of General Sheridan's personal mess wagon, was one of those delegated to go after the calf. Being a teamster and not an enlisted soldier, young Murphy did not think he needed a pass to get through the picket lines. Intercepted, he was reported to Custer. Custer ordered the boy sent to the guard house and made to carry a log until Custer should order him discharged from this punishment.

There was no actual guard house, an open space in camp serving in that capacity. Selecting a chunk of wood Johnny began his sentence. Throughout the night and all the next day the boy continued. Custer apparently had forgotten him. The third day was Christmas. That day was half gone, with the boy still marching around carrying the log on his shoulder, when Sheridan chanced to pass that way. The General inquired the cause of such a spectacle. Johnny explained.

Murphy's own recital of what happened after that is worth quoting:[1]

> His (Sheridan's) exclamation which followed would not bear repetition here. Things happened pretty fast then. I never saw the General walk as rapidly, either before or afterward, as he did when he went to call successively upon the wagonmaster, the master of transportation, the officer of the day and General Custer.

An occurance during his Black Hills expedition in 1873 further illustrates Custer's barbaric attitude even toward his own men. One day while Custer was writing in his tent, one of his Indian scouts entered to register a complaint. Annoyed at the interruption, Custer sprang to his feet and slugged the surprised intruder about the face so severely that his companions threatened trouble when he returned to them with his visage badly battered and explained what had happened.

They demanded that Custer, himself, go to the guard house, there to accept the same kind of punishment he was so accustomed to inflict upon others who engaged in like brawls.

Instead of attempting to appease the Indians, Custer chose to make his victim's lot even worse. He told Bloody Knife, Crow leader of the Indian scouts, that he had punished this man for going over his chief's head, so to speak, intimating that the man had done so in a deliberate attempt to humiliate Bloody Knife. For a long time Custer worked on Bloody Knife's vanity and jealousy. Finally, that

1. "Reminiscences of the Washita Campaign," Chronicles of Oklahoma, Vol. 1, page 264.

worthy went back to his followers and prevailed upon them to flog the hapless, helpless Indian unmercifully with their heavy buffalo quirts.

To quote Custer's most eulogistic biographer, Captain Frederick Whitaker: [2]

> A few moments later, all the Indians rushed to the quarters where the poor sufferer was in bed, nursed by his friends, pulled him out and commenced lashing him with their heavy buffalo whips, the chief being the heaviest in his blows. The innate sense of necessity of subordination in military society was aroused. Even the wild savage could see the force of Custer's lucid argument.

Strictly devoid of vices and evil habits during his earlier days, Custer became a heavy drinker and fast liver during the Civil War. Then, as suddenly, he quit dissipations. Thereafter, he was severe on any officer or enlisted man of his command who drank to excess.

Extremely modest as a young man, Custer grew vain later. During the war between the states he took delight in donning outlandish costumes. At times, however, he was meticulous in his personal attire. One distinctive feature of his personal appearance was his long, curly, flaxen hair which seldom was subjected to the barber's shears. One outstanding exception was at the time of marriage. Then he suffered his locks to be shorn. He also submitted to a tonsorial operation shortly before setting forth on his last campaign into the land of the Sioux. In some of the most important engagements of the Civil War he wore a wide brimmed plantation sombrero of straw, and in others a ragged felt, instead of the regulation headdress. During his life on the plains he varied his dress between civilian garb, the habiliments of his rank and buckskins. His vanity, his desire to appear distinctive, led him to

2. Captain Frederick Whitaker's "Popular Life of Custer," page 618.

don whatever dress would make him most conspicuous and distinguish him from his companions.

Custer had a penchant for writing. During his
Civil War career his official reports were modest.
Not so the letters he wrote to his friends and relatives. In later years his narratives of his life on
the Plains were couched in a style pretending to reflect an unpretentious nature, yet the adroitness
of his diction invariably impressed the reader with
Custer's great prowess as a hunter and fighter. Unfortunately for these hapless red men who offered
armed protest to violation of sacred treaties by
white men, Custer's highly colored narrative of his
conquests gave to the world the impression that all
Plains Indians were vicious, uncouth, bloodthirsty
savages deserving the merciless fate such barbaric
militarists as Custer meted out to them. Only in
recent years has this impression been successfully
reversed.

No one given to "reading between the lines"
can read Custer's own works on the Washita campaign without discovering that romance as well as
adventure injected itself into Custer's experiences
during this expedition. There are many enthusias-
tic allusions to the physical attractions of the Indian maiden, Monahseetah, scattered throughout his
memoirs.[3] He carried her with him as an "in-
interpreter," although she spoke no English, from the
time he left Camp Supply on his return to the Washita until he quit his command at Fort Hays four
months later when he took leave of her as his wife
joined him at that place. Such things give the reader grounds for considerable speculation in regard
to their relationships during this period.

Monahseetah was one of the Indian girls carried
away from Black Kettle's village among Custer's

3. Custer's "Life on the Plains," pages 249 and 316.

women captives. She was the daughter of Little Rock, second to Black Kettle in rank among the chieftains of that village. Little Rock was killed in the Washita massacre. Custer admits the maiden preferred his company to that of her own people during the four months he had her with him. This preference on her part, he said, made it unnecessary to place a guard over her movements, even when they were in the field and in close proximity to her tribe.

Magpie and Little Beaver remembered Monahseetah well. She was a little older than they, in her later 'teens, at the time she fell into Custer's hands. Magpie said the Cheyennes had little use for her after her return to the tribe when Custer went north for good because she had displayed a preference for her captor so long as he would keep her with him.

Kish Hawkins also knew her and her history. So did John Otterby. Hawkins was serving as interpreter for the writer when Little Beaver was interrogated regarding his mother's account of mistreatment of Indian women prisoners the first night after they arrived in Camp Supply. His mother, Little Beaver said, asserted this girl was Custer's selection on that occasion and that a mutual friendship seemed to spring up between them immediately. She gave birth to a child during the following summer while still a captive at Fort Hays. The papoose was yellow-haired and fair skinned.

Monahseetah named him "Yellow Swallow."

She knew Custer as "Yellow Hair."

CHAPTER TWO

Black Kettle and Other Chiefs

$\mathcal{I}$N his Washita campaign Custer was destined to encounter the flower of Plains knighthood, those chiefs whose qualifications as warriors, diplomats and statesmen entitled them to a much more kindly fate than was in store for them.

Martyr of the Battle of the Washita was Black Kettle. The white man's conquest of the Western Prairies presents no more tragically heroic character than this great Cheyenne chieftain who fell at the first burst of bullets Custer's immediate command unloosed that fateful November morning as it dashed across the icy Washita.

Mighty hunter, daring warrior, wise in council, he was the most renowned of all the great leaders who lifted the Cheyennes to preeminence among the wild tribes. Not only was he first in war, but he was first in peace. Without his personal sacrifices, his constant efforts to avoid hostilities, his firm leashing of warlike spirits, the confidence placed in his diplomatic dealings with the invading whites, not only by his own people, but also by other tribes, the story of the subjugation of the western frontier would have been far more sanguinary than it is.

Black Kettle's assassination well may be considered the blackest blotch, an indelible smear against the brilliant military record of General Custer. It is one chapter all historians would have spared the story of the winning of the West; but faithfulness to fact demands that it be included.

Black Kettle earned his right to be regarded the greatest chief the Cheyennes possessed, one of the greatest Indian leaders that ever roamed the plains, the most influential in his day from the Dominion to the Rio Grande. He had earned undying fame on the warpath long before Custer was born. Eighteen years prior to the Battle of the Washita he was one of the most celebrated of Cheyenne war chiefs. Those were the days when the Pawnees were looked upon by most contemporaries as the scourge of the Plains. Numerically strong and possessed of good mounts, they constantly were sending strong war parties from their own territory in what is now Nebraska to prey upon their rivals. For nearly thirty years they and the Cheyennes had been constant enemies. And far back, in 1853, Black Kettle was accorded the honor of carrying the sacred Cheyenne arrows into one of the most important battles between these two tribes. Such service was a mark of distinction, for the Sacred Arrows were the most potent of all Cheyenne medicines. Their capture meant disaster, hence they were entrusted to only the bravest of the brave and the most accomplished warriors.

Eight years after this notable engagement Black Kettle had achieved such prestige among his people as to be one of the principal chiefs called into council when the Government sought to have them yield their choicest hunting ground. On this occasion he refused to sign. He did not feel that the Indians were being dealt with fairly. He considered this a matter of such grave importance as to require sanction of a majority of the members of the tribe, not one to be decided by a few.

This was the beginning of Black Kettle's prestige in peace councils. From that time forth, for the remainder of his lifetime, he was the leading peace commissioner of the red men of the Southern Plains. While a stickler for the rights of his people, he always was a leading advocate of the policy of settling

John Metcalf

Drawn From Photograph

BLACK KETTLE

differences between the Government and Indians by diplomacy rather than by force. Always he was able to prevail upon his associates to yield slightly more than they wanted to, rather than invite further bloodshed by needless stubbornness. Always Black Kettle wanted peace for all the tribes, as well as for his own. He recognized their common claim to the prairies. He soon learned from bitter experience, however, that the white man would punish all for the overt acts of a few, regardless of individual or tribal responsibility.

His recognized preeminence among chiefs of the associated tribes and his understanding of the magnitude of his responsibilities, as well as his earnest desire to avoid clashes with the invading white forces, are strikingly illustrated by the following letter he dispatched to Agent Colley at Fort Lyon only a few weeks before the Sand Creek massacre:[1]

> We received a letter from Bent wishing us to make peace. We held a council in regard to it. All come to the conclusion to make peace with you, providing that you make peace with the Kiowas, Comanches, Arapahoes, Apaches and Sioux. We are going to send a messenger to the Kiowas and to the other nations about our going to make peace with you. We hear that you have some (Indian) prisoners in Denver. We have seven prisoners of yours which we are willing to give up, providing you give up yours. There are three (Cheyenne) war parties yet out and two Arapahoes. They have been out for some time and are expected in soon. When we held council there were few Arapahoes and Sioux present. We want true news from you in return. This is a letter.
>
> (Signed) BLACK KETTLE AND OTHER CHIEFS

Signatures of the other chiefs were immaterial. All recognized that that of Black Kettle was the only name necessary.

This letter brought results. It brought Major

1. Report of Commissioner of Indian Affairs, 1865, page 233.

E. W. Wynkoop, commandant at Fort Lyon, to the Cheyenne village to receive the prisoners and to arrange for a peace council in Denver. It took Black Kettle and other chiefs on a four hundred mile pilgrimage to Denver and back to their people, a pilgrimage the Indians thought resulted in a definite, peaceful settlement of the current difficulties. But actually it led to the massacre of several of these chiefs and hundreds of their followers a few weeks later by the same officer to whom they had looked for security, believing he had promised them protection if they would separate themselves from the hostiles.

It also led to the temporary retirement of Black Kettle as head of the Cheyenne nation and recognition of another in his stead; but in less than a year's time he had been restored to supremacy, in time to place his name first on the peace treaty of 1865.

Scrapping of this treaty by the Government again weakened Black Kettle's prestige with his own people. It was with the greatest difficulty he was able to drag them back for another treaty effort in 1867. Soon thereafter assassination by Custer on the Washita ended his career.

Perhaps there could be no greater testimonial to the high rating of Black Kettle than the eagerness of all soldiers and their Indian allies to claim the distinction of having slain this famed chieftain. This in spite of the fact that Black Kettle was the outstanding exponent of peace among all the so-called wild tribesmen. To have killed him was the boast of braggarts made falsely on two occasions previous to the time of his actual death.

In the spring of 1864, Lieutenant George Eayre was sent with a detachment in search of a band of Cheyennes who were suspected of having run off some stock belonging to a Government contractor. His troops clashed with a band of Indians. Several on each side were killed. In making his report, Eayre said Black Kettle was among those slain. This was in April.

In November of that same year, Colonel J. M. Chivington attacked Black Kettle's camp in Southern Colorado. His dispatch sent that night to General S. R. Curtis at Fort Leavenworth included this statement: "We killed Chiefs Black Kettle, White Antelope and Little Robe and between four and five hundred other Indians."

As a matter of fact, neither Black Kettle nor Little Robe was among those slaughtered on that occasion.

At the close of the Washita massacre, Trotter, one of Custer's Osage trailers, exhibited a scalp which he said was that of Black Kettle. He boasted he had engaged Black Kettle in hand-to-hand combat and, after a terrific struggle, had slain the Cheyenne leader.

Once again this claim was disproved, for no one engaged Black Kettle in hand-to-hand combat on the Washita and his scalp was not taken.

Many of Black Kettle's contemporaries, on the hunt, on the warpath, and in peace councils, also were his neighbors along the Washita. They also were destined to become victims of Custer's perfidy, although most of them escaped death at his hands during the Washita campaign.

Notable among them were Little Raven and Yellow Bear of the Arapahoes, Satanta, Satank, Lone Wolf and Kicking Bird of the Kiowas, Little Robe, Little Rock and Medicine Arrow of the Cheyennes.

As far back as the early 'Fifties, Little Raven was one of the most influential war chiefs among the Arapahoes. In 1854 the Plains Indians united to war against the eastern tribes then encroaching upon their favorite hunting grounds. These invaders had killed many Cheyennes, Kiowas, Comanches and Arapahoes. Little Raven headed the Arapahoe contingent which went forth to avenge these deaths and to attempt to turn back this invasion. Six years later he represented his people in a peace council at Bent's Fort. His name is the first of the Arapahoes signing the Little Arkansas treaty of 1865 as well as the Medicine Lodge treaty of 1867.

Like Black Kettle, Little Raven always was an advocate of peace with the Whites but always he was adamant in his demand that the Indians be treated fairly. In one respect he overshadowed his illustrious Cheyenne contemporary. He was a more accomplished orator. As a result, it generally was Little Raven who served as chief spokesman for the Indians at such conferences. Of his forensic abilities one who sat in on the Medicine Lodge conference wrote: [2]

> Towering above all in native intellect and oratory—
> exact image of Andrew Johnson, barring his color—
> Little Raven, chief of the Arapahoes, was there. His
> speech before the commission on the question of
> damages, back annuities and the cause of the war
> would have done credit to any enlightened statesman.
> His reference to the Chivington massacre and ill
> treatment the Indians had received at the hands of
> white men of the frontier, who, he alleged, had been
> constantly infringing upon their reservation rights in
> the past, were scathing, and his plea for protection
> and better treatment in the future was the most touch-
> ing piece of impassioned oratory to which the writtr
> ever listened, before or since.

Little Raven continued his leadership and diplomatic representations long after Custer had gone from the Washita and the Plains tribes had settled upon their reservations, yet had failed to get justice from the White Father. He was spokesmen for them

2. Alfred A. Taylor's "The Medicine Lodge Peace Council," in "Chronicles of Oklahoma," Vol II, page 113.

when a protesting delegation went to Washington
for a personal conference with the president and to
appeal to the citizenship of the East for justice.

It was Little Raven's Arapahoes, first village below that of Black Kettle on the Washita, which cut
off Major Elliott's retreat, making it possible for
the allied tribesmen to annihilate this detachment
while Custer was sacking Black Kettle's camp only
two miles away. Little Raven's followers also were
among those who chased Custer away from the
Washita that night. It was several weeks after
that before Little Raven would trust his people within sight of white soldiers and then only after exact-
ing a promise from General Sheridan that Custer
would not be permitted to molest them.

Next in rank to Little Raven among the Arapahoes was Yellow Bear. He, too, was both warrior
and diplomat, willing to go to any reasonable length
to prevent continuation of warfare between the Indians and Whites.

Satanta was to the Kiowas of that period what
Little Raven was to the Arapahoes and Black Kettle
was to the Cheyennes. At that time he was about
fifty years old. He had earned his place at the head
of his tribe by virtue of his prowess as a warrior
and his firm, brilliant record as a representative
in peace councils. Though Little Raven may have
excelled him in the Medicine Lodge pact negotiations so far as forensic performance is concerned,
nevertheless Satanta was known throughout the nation as "the orator of the Plains."

Satanta's constant associate was Lone Wolf, a
leader whose rise to prominence among his people
had been gained as a war chief rather than as a
diplomat. Lone Wolf was hereditary chief of the
Kiowas. Throughout the conquest of the Southern
Plains, Lone Wolf's fortunes and those of Satanta
were strikingly parallel. Later he was among the

Plains Indian leaders who were exiled to Florida in an effort to break up sporadic rebellions against the constant encroachment of the Whites on the lands and rights of the red men of the South.

Villages of Satanta and Lone Wolf were far below the main concentration on the Washita at the time of the Black Kettle massacre. Both Satanta and Lone Wolf were sleeping in General Hazen's tent at Fort Cobb at the time, having gone there to obtain supplies.³ Later Custer seized these two chiefs, when they approached him on a peaceful mission, and held them as hostages to force submission of their followers who yielded only on threat of the execution of their beloved chiefs.

This mistreatment and others of a similar nature were responsible for Satanta leading raiding parties into Texas a year or two later. On one of these raids the wagon-master and six teamsters of a Government freighting train were killed. When a number of Indians were arrested for this act, Satanta went to Fort Sill and attempted to take all the blame upon himself. In typical, dramatic language, he told his listeners:

"If any other Indian claims the honor of leading that party, he is not talking straight.   Satanta led it."

But, despite Satanta's willingness to accept full responsibility, Big Tree, one of his companions on

---

3. Several years after the Battle of the Washita, General Hazen wrote a lengthy "Some Corrections of Life on the Plains," which was published in full in "Chronicles of Oklahoma," Vol. III, page 295. These "corrections" contradicted many of the assertions made by both Sheridan and Custer, especially in regard to participation by Kiowas and Comanches. On page 306 is found the following: "My retained return of provisions shows that on the 26th (of November, 1868) . . . I issued rations to nine-tenths of all the Kiowas under my charge. And that night, Satanta, Satank, Lone Wolf and nearly all of the main Kiowa chiefs slept in my tent. I had breakfast prepared for them, and they left their camp next morning, the 27th, about 10 or 11 o'clock, several hours after the battle was fought."

SATANTA

that expedition, was convicted with him and both
of them were sentenced, by a cowboy jury, to be
hanged at Jacksboro, Texas. Knowing how badly
Satanta had been mistreated by Custer, many in-
terceded for the two men, bringing such pressure to
bear upon the Texas authorities that their sentences
were commuted to life imprisonment. Parole followed. Not long thereafter Satanta was rearrested,
accused of fomenting trouble among the reservation
tribes, and his parole was revoked. After brooding
for months over what he considered the injustice
done him and his people, and, after being convinced
that he could never remedy their condition, he took
his own life by leaping from a window on the second
floor of the prison hospital at Huntsville, Texas.

While Custer's vindicative pen painted Satanta
a vicious savage, the general's contemporaries did
not find him such. In the spring of 1864, H. T. Ketch-
am, a medical missionary, was sent among the Upper Arkansas Indians whose ranks were being ravished by an epidemic of smallpox. His duties carried him into Satanta's village and lodge. Of his
experiences there he wrote:[4]

> I was four days in Satanta's, or White Bear's village,
> who is, I believe, their principal chief. He is a fine
> looking Indian, very energetic and as sharp as a
> briar. He and all his people treated me with much
> friendship. I ate meals three times a day in his
> lodge. He puts on a great deal of style; spreads a
> carpet for his guests to sit on and has painted five
> boards, twenty inches wide and three feet long, or-
> namented with bright brass tacks driven all around
> the edges, which they use for tables. He has a brass
> French horn which he blew vigorously when meals
> were ready.

That Satanta possessed a keen sense of humor,
a sound understanding of the Indians' rights, and a
highly developed knowledge of argument is evi-
denced by a statement he made to an investigating
commission sent to the Plains by Congress, follow-

ing Custer's Washita campaign. Satanta said:[5]

> We have tried the white man's road and find it hard. We find nothing on it but a little corn which hurts our teeth. No sugar, no coffee, but we still want to walk the white man's road.
>
> We want to have guns, breach-loading carbines, ammunition and caps. These are part of the white man's road, yet you want us to go back to making arrowheads which are used only by bad, foolish Indians and have always been a mark of what was barbarous and evil. We want civilized weapons to hunt with. You want us to go back to savage ones.

Kicking Bird, like Lone Wolf, was a younger Kiowa chieftain. He was one of the few Kiowas to actualy clash with Custer at the time of the Black Kettle fight. His small band participated in the closing acts of that tragedy. His band was one of the last to yield, but, having made up his mind that the welfare of his people demanded submission, he became such an advocate of peace that he aroused the animosities of many of his contemporaries. He died suddenly, believed to have been poisoned by those who thought he was too friendly with the Whites.

Such were the Indian leaders against whom Custer was to operate.

Yet Custer called them barbarians—savages.

4. Report of Commissioner of Indian Affairs, 1864, page 258.

5. Report of Commissioner of Indian Affairs, 1869, page 61.

CHAPTER THREE

Creating New War Clouds

*A*LL was quiet on the Western frontier. Indian fury, fired to unprecedented savagery by Colonel Chivington's brutal massacre of peaceable Cheyennes on Sand Creek in Southern Colorado less than three years previously, had spent its force.[1] The red man's raids of retaliation had ravished the frontier from Smoky Hill River to the Black Hills. Wagon trains had been plundered. So had stage stations. Transcontinental travel had been paralyzed. Stock had been driven from isolated ranches. Lives of hundreds of white soldiers, teamsters and white settlers had atoned for Chivington's wanton slaughter.

Their thirst for revenge having been satiated, avenging hordes had quit the warpath to retire peaceably to those inviolate hunting grounds set aside for them under the treaty signed on the banks of the Little Arkansas River in the early autumn of 1865.

The road to California and Oregon once more was open. Peaceful trading had been reestablished. Once again settlers were flocking into the territory ceded to the white man in exchange for pledges that the red man would not be molested in those areas set aside for his exclusive use.

Northern Cheyennes, Northern Arapahoes, and the Sioux had withdrawn from overland trails.

To avoid further trouble with the Whites, Black Kettle's Southern Cheyennes, other groups of that

1. See Appendix A.

same tribe headed by Seven Bulls, Little Robe, Medicine Arrow and Black White Man, Arapahoes under Little Raven, Storm, Big Mouth, Spotted Wolf, had retired south of the Arkansas, even before the close of northern raiding.

Only the Dog Soldiers, most implacable division of the Cheyennes, were disgruntled. They had refused to sign the treaty of 1865 because it required them to give up their favorite hunting grounds along the Republican and Smoky Hill rivers. But they were merely sullen, rather than actively hostile. Kiowas, too, under Lone Wolf, Satanta' and Satank had been unusually quiet south of the Arkansas. Comparatively few inconsequental raids into Texas recently had marred tranquility of that region.

While the Indians thus were attempting to adjust themselves to the new order of things, willing to go to any reasonable limit that they might hunt and dwell in harmony with their unwelcome neighbors, new strife was being fomented by the invaders. Soon the red man was to become the hapless victim of an old feud between contentious factions of the Whites, the War Department and the Interior Department.

Close of the Civil War, two years previously, had brought reorganization of the Federal army. Scores of ambitious officers had been reduced in rank and had been deprived of an opportunity to distinguish themselves in action. Ambitions born during the closing months of war between the states suddenly had been nullified. Many craved action. Where? Activities against the Plains Indians offered the only prospect.

For more than a year there had been open hostility between the Interior Department and the War Department over the frontier situation. Indian agents insisted their charges craved permanent peace, pointing to their repeated surrender of lands and further retirement from the lanes of Plains commerce as proof of this desire. Militarists warned that the Indian agents were being duped. They magnified every overt act on the part of an Indian. Minor raids by small, unattached bands frequently were heralded as forerunners of a general uprising. They argued the only way to settle the Indian question was by armed subjugation; by forcing at the point of the bayonet every Plains Indian to give up his nomadic life and to settle down to the white man's mode of living within the confines of restrictive reservations.

The break came late in the Winter of 1866-67. In spite of the fact that there had been less trouble with the Indians than at any time in recent years, those seeking war insisted this merely was a lull before an impending storm. They professed to have reliable information that as soon as the greening grass of spring should enable the red man's war ponies to regain strength lost through scant forage of winter, the Indians planned to make a concerted raid on all frontier settlements, stage lines and freighting trails. Furthermore, there was the Kansas Pacific railroad which had been projected as far as Fort Riley. According to plans of its builders, it was to be pushed another hundred miles into the Indian country during the ensuing twelve months. It was argued that this thrust would bring opposition from the Indians unless a strong show of military force could be made in the meantime.

Under guise of establishing this protective force, General Hancock was assigned to command the Division of the Missouri and was authorized to organize an expedition against any hostiles who might threaten operations in Western Kansas.

Most effective unit of the Hancock Expedition was to be the Seventh Cavalry regiment. While nominal direction was vested in Colonel A. J. Smith, a veteran officer who had been named to command when this regiment was authorized six months previously, Lieutenant Colonel George A. Custer was charged with actual recruiting, drilling and leadership.

This was a welcome assignment for the fiery young cavalryman who had distinguished himself during the closing months of the Civil War. He had obtained a taste of Plains life while on duty in Texas the previous year. He had become bored by inactivity. He welcomed this opportunity to swing back into active service. It gratified his adventurous spirit to operate against a wily foe which had disconcerted all army leaders who heretofore had endeavored to match it in Plains warfare. Furthermore, after being mustered out of the volunteer service, following his brief term of duty in Texas, his pay had been reduced from $8,000 a year and a liberal allowance for subsistence to only $2,000 with a greatly curtailed living account. His mode of living demanded more than his peace-time stipend.

Custer lost no time assembling, organizing and grooming the cavalry unit destined soon to seize the spotlight and hold it for an entire decade. The Seventh Cavalry was only a skeleton regiment when he took charge, a skeleton of unsound material. Like most of the regulars, a majority of these soldiers had led a life of idleness and dissipation since the close of the Civil War. Rigid discipline cured some, ousted others. Custer filled in with recruits, green, so far as military tactics were concerned, but the great majority of them were rough and ready individuals. They were more or less fitted by nature, even though some of them were city bred, for the service ahead, as soon as they could be schooled in the soldiering methods required for fighting Plains Indians.

In this respect, not even Custer, himself, held much of an advantage, as his experiences soon were to prove. He soon was to discover that West Point tacticians knew nothing of the Plains method of fighting, that there is a great deal of difference between leading a sabre charge against a massed body of troops and attempting to get within striking distance of the phantom warriors of the prairies. Nowhere in the record of nearly ten years he spent on the frontier is it recorded that Custer ever did learn how to match fighting prowess with the elusive foemen who eventually annihilated him and with him the flower of this same Seventh Cavalry.

But, by sheer determination, rigorous discipline and tireless energy he had the Seventh whipped into shape to give a better account of itself than any other outfit of Hancock's command when that expedition set forth in April to rid Western Kansas of a fancied Indian menace.

Seven companies of infantry, helpless, hopeless, ineffective soldiers for such a mission, a pontoon train, a battery of artillery and four companies of Custer's cavalry comprised the expeditionary force which departed Fort Riley the last week in March. At Fort Harker two more troops of cavalry were added. Supplies were picked up here and, despite protests from Colonel J. H. Leavenworth, agent of the Kiowas and Comanches, that all Indians in that region were friendly, the expedition moved on to Fort Larned. There Colonel Wynkoop, agent for the Cheyennes and Arapahoes, added his protestations to those of Colonel Leavenworth—without avail. Militarists held the upper hand in Washington, at least for the moment. Control of the Plains by force, rather than by diplomacy, had been decreed. Those in power were not to be dissuaded from carrying out the orders for which they had waited so long and so eagerly.

At Fort Zarah, where Hancock rested on his march from Fort Harker to Fort Larned, he had learned some five hundred lodges of Indians were encamped on Pawnee Fork—less than fifty miles from Larned. He promptly determined to make this immense village his first goal, even though there had been no recent depredations of any nature in that vicinity. White prisoners had been taken by some Kiowas in Texas. That sufficed. Indians were Indians to most of the military leaders operating on the Plains. Regardless of who the offenders were, it was common practice to take the nearest red man to task for any offense committed anywhere by any Indian.

Advised by Agent Wynkoop that General Hancock desired a conference with them, some of the chiefs braved a belated snow to ride this long distance and counsel with the soldier leader. Contrary to the custom of holding friendly councils in the daytime, Hancock insisted on a night conference, an incident inclined to arouse suspicions of the Indians. They believed evil spirits hovered over any council upon which the sun did not shine. Hancock's demand that they procure the release of white prisoners held by the Kiowas further tended to convince these chiefs that the soldiers were deliberately unreasonable, determined to find some pretext for attacking their village.

Their fears were aroused still further next day when, upon resuming his march, Hancock quitted the main trail and moved up Pawnee Fork toward their camp. Nor did Hancock's demand that more chiefs come to see him for another conference tend to assure them. Suggestion of Roman Nose that this might be a trick to get them within the soldiers' power found many credulous listeners. His further suggestion that a considerable force go forth to meet the approaching soldiers, prepared for any eventuality should negotiations prove unsatisfactory, was adopted.

It was an uneasy village that waited, wondered and watched as the leading chiefs, Roman Nose and a number of other warriors set forth. Sand Creek still was fresh in their memories. They still could see children ruthlessly shot down, women vulgarly mutiliated, ghastly corpses of warriors who had died in defense of the helpless, scalped, mangled, strewn over the ground or heaped in gruesome piles. Ashes where lodges had stood floated in memory before them. That tragedy had struck their people from skies as peaceful as those of the present. Did these approaching soldiers plan a similar fate for this village? These warriors were determined not to be caught off guard.

Gloomily the red man's cavalcade moved to meet that of the white man. Gloom was not caused by doubt of their own ability to cope with the plodding soldiers in actual battle. It was concern for their families. It was disappointment that their hopes of permanent peace, as pledged by each race in the treaty councils on the Little Arkansas, seemed certain of being dashed. Certainly such a large force of troops, whose leader seemed determined to goad Indians to desperation, augured ill. The white chief appeared determined to pick a quarrel.

But they would face the issue bravely and without any display of weakness. They would put on a bold front when they met their unwelcome guests. All were decked out in their finest.

Since the soldier chief seemed to be the one and only source of contention, Roman Nose proposed to his associates that he take it upon himself to single out Hancock and kill him.[2] With Hancock eliminated, peace might be maintained. To this, the chiefs objected. Such an act, they pointed out, would be just what their enemies wanted. It would prevent

2. George Bird Grinnell's "Fighting Cheyennes," page 241.

their friends, such as Agent Wynkoop and Agent Leavenworth, holding in check those so eager to start a new war.

As the two columns came within sight of each other, chiefs and headmen spread out in front of the other warriors. It was a colorful and brave display. Back of them came their followers, and still farther in the rear rode a scattered few, ready to bear quick news to the village should hostilities be started.

Suddenly there was a stir at the far end of the approaching column of soldiers. There the cavalry had been marching. Infantry, artillery and pioneers had formed ahead for the march. At breakneck speed and with sabres drawn, the horsemen rushed to the front and swung into line of battle, Custer at their head.

To those eager messengers who rode far in rear of the Indian lines, it looked like battle. Without waiting to see the outcome, they dashed away to give the alarm in the village. Flight of non-combatants commenced immediately, fugitives taking with them only such articles as they could carry easily and which would not hamper them in making a quick get-away. Lodges were left standing.

But it was not to fight. While still quite a distance apart, the rival lines halted. From one side rode forward a group of officers; from the other Roman Nose and chiefs. Once More Roman Nose declared his intentions of shooting General Hancock as soon as they met. Again he was restrained.

Apparently those with Hancock who knew Roman Nose had pointed him out to the general, for, as the emissaries came face to face, Hancock addressed himself to this warrior instead of to any of the chiefs.[3] Roman Nose glared steadfastly into the general's face for some little time.

3. While Roman Nose was one of the most famous Cheyenne warriors of all time, he never was a chief.

"Do the Indians want war?" boomed Hancock's challenge.

Roman Nose continued to look him straight in the eye with ill-concealed hostility, not far removed from contempt. In steady, measured tones he replied:

"If Indian wanted war, would he bring few warriors so close to so many soldiers; so close to big guns."

Then Hancock demanded:

"Why did not Roman Nose come to the council when I sent for him before?"

Back came the modulated answer:

"Roman Nose's horses not strong enough to make long ride. Besides, Roman Nose afraid soldier chief not talk straight."

Then the talk shifted to the others, Bull Bear, head of the Dog Soldiers doing most of the speaking for the Indians. He urged Hancock not to come any nearer the camp for fear of alarming the village.

"Indian remember Sand Creek when soldiers come up like this and try to kill everybody. Our women and children are afraid of soldiers," he said.

Pawnee Killer of the Sioux and White Horse of the Cheyennes added their voices to this protest.

But Hancock was not acquiescent. He reiterated his intention of moving up close before pitching camp. Until then, he said with finality, there would be no further discussion of the subject.

Back toward their village turned the Indians. The soldier column resumed its march.

Shortly Hancock saw some of his recent visitors approaching again. They came to report that the village, alarmed by approach of such a large body of troops and fearing an attack was imminent, had fled.

Here, indeed, was disappointing news to the general. He pondered a moment, then said:

"Go, bring your people back. Tell them to return to their lodges. They will not be harmed."

Then he ordered the column to go into camp.

While tents were being erected, Hancock sent for Edmund Guerrier, a half-breed Cheyenne scout and interpreter. He sent for Custer. He instructed Guerrier to enter the village, ascertain the exact situation and report. He ordered Custer to surround the village with his cavalry as soon as night should fall, and, as soon as this encircling movement had been completed, to attack. He doubted the inhabitants had fled. If they had, he believed their chiefs would bring them back. In either case, he expected to seize all.

For hours the soldiers prepared for their first clash with Indians. Loose shoes on horses were tightened. Those missing were replaced. Guns were inspected carefully to see that they were loaded and ready for service. Extra ammunition was obtained from the supply train and stored in saddlebags.

With greatest caution the village was surrounded after darkness had come. At a given signal the troops moved forward. They swept into the lodges unchallenged. Examination showed the tepees were empty. The Indians had not been deceived by Hancock's promise of security. Those on Sand Creek also had been assured of their safety, only to be attacked and massacred. Pawnee Killer, White Horse, Roman Nose and their associates had profited by this previous display of bad faith on the part of soldiers. All were far away when Custer closed in.

Saying the infantry would look out for the village, General Hancock ordered Custer to give pursuit to the fleeing Indians as soon as it should be light enough to pick up the trail.

Before dawn the men were in their saddles and on the trail. It was not hard to find nor difficult to follow, at first, at a rapid pace. It headed west.

Across Walnut creek it led and still westward, then north, easily discernable for awhile. Then it grew dimmer and smaller. Soon it faded entirely. More than one thousand Indians were gone without leaving a trace which even experienced trailers could follow. They had broken into small bands to be reunited either in part or in full at a prearranged point or points.

Their goal was the wild hunting grounds along the Republican and Smoky Hill rivers.

Nothing was left for Custer to do but to go into camp for the night, send word of his failure to Hancock and prepare to resume the search by detachments on the morrow.

From that time forth, Custer, not Hancock, was to do the campaigning. Henceforth, Custer was to be the dominating figure in Plains warfare.

But for the remainder of this summer the conquest was doomed to dismal failure. While Custer roamed that region hunting for hostiles, never to encounter them, the Indians raided stagelines and settlements. When an accounting was made that autumn, three hundred whites—soldiers, teamsters and settlers—had paid with their lives for the treachery of Hancock and Custer. Only four Indians had been killed. The war had cost the Government nine million dollars!

Only two of the Indians killed could be credited to Custer's men. Here is how:

In the village on Pawnee Fork at the time of Hancock's approach were six members of Black Kettle's Cheyennes. They had come from Black Kettle's village, located far to the south, to visit friends. They had left their ponies south of the river. Had they expected trouble, they would have brought their horses on into the village with them. As Hancock's column appeared, they set out afoot to return to their horses and to their own people.

They had not gene far when one suggested that they turn aside toward a nearby stage station where they might be able to pick up some mounts. On the way thither they encountered one of Custer's scouting parties. They fled toward a stream, were overtaken while crossing, were fired upon and two were killed. The others escaped to carry word south of the beginning of a new war thrust upon them by the military.

Twelve soldier lives was the price paid for the other two Indians killed during the summer. These soldiers were sacrificed by General Sherman who had come into the field in a vain attempt to turn the conflagration, which Hancock and Custer had started, into a prairie fire that would consume all Indians in that region. From his headquarters at Fort Sedgewick on the Platte, General Sherman started dispatches to Custer, then on the Republican. They were entrusted to Lieutenant Kidder. Kidder was given an escort of ten troopers and a friendly Sioux, Red Bead, as a guide. Arriving at Custer's old camp after the Seventh had moved out, Kidder attempted to follow south to Fort Wallace.

Near Beaver Creek, the Kidder party was sighted by some of Pawnee Killer's Sioux. These, with a few Cheyennes, were hunting buffalo in that region. A war party immediately was organized to go after these soldiers.

First to sight the soldiers was a small group of a dozen Cheyennes. The troopers were moving along at a leisurely trot. Discovering they were being followed, they increased their pace to a gallop. But they could not distance the fleet ponies of their pursuers. Kidder halted his men in a ravine, dismounted them, and forming them in a circle, prepared to fight it out in white man fashion.

Ordinarily the Indians would have fought cautiously, once they had their foes at their mercy.

INDIAN TERRITORY IN 1868

They seldom take unnecessary risks and they might have wiped out this group without loss to themselves. But it so happened that Tobacco was one of the Cheyennes engaged. And Tobacco was supposed to bear a charmed life. His protective medicine was an oddly shaped warclub, which, according to the tradition which came to him with it, rendered its possessor invulnerable. This same tradition demanded that its possessor perform deeds of valor in keeping with the knowledge that he could not be harmed.

So Tobacco rode bravely in, discharging his rifle in the very faces of the little circle. Around and around the huddled dozen he rode, firing and reloading and firing again. Not to be outdone, others followed. Within a few minutes the little band of troopers was the center of a moving ring of death. Sioux joined the Cheyennes to pour bullets and arrows into its ranks. Eventually the last man was killed.

Then the Indians dashed in. It was the first time Pawnee Killer's braves had obtained a good chance to register vengeance on soldiers for burning their village. Two of their number had just fallen. This called for further revenge. They stripped every body, mutilated the corpses and, before departing, rode by, shooting arrows into them. When Custer eventually found this missing detachment, the bodies were fairly bristling with shafts.

Had soldiers scored a similar victory, Custer's narrative would have set it down as a "glorious victory in fair fight." Being an Indian triumph, he termed it a "massacre." And this "Kidder Massacre" soon became one of the incidents by which Custer sought to justify his merciless persecutions of a later day.

It was during his search for Lieutenant Kidder and party and subsequent events after his arrival at Fort Wallace that Custer became guilty of acts which brought court-martial, his second, at the close of the campaign.

Having received no pay for a long time, having been forced by Custer's utter disregard for the physical endurance of either man or beast to make long, hard marches on scant rations, thirteen members of his command quit camp in broad daylight. Seven were mounted and six were on foot. No sooner had Custer recovered from his astonishment at this bold desertion than he ordered them to be brought back, dead or alive. His own narrative admits his orders left the impression he preferred their dead bodies to living effective soldiers.

Pursuing troops under Major Elliott were unable to overtake the mounted men, but they did overhaul those on foot. Orders to halt being ignored, the troops opened fire, killing one and wounding two others. The remainder gave up. This was count "one."

After his arrival at Fort Wallace, Custer decided to go to Fort Riley to visit his wife. Without obtaining permission from the proper superior, he went to Fort Riley.

These two acts brought his conviction by a court-martial which sentenced him to be relieved of duty without pay for a year.

It was during this enforced vacation that he returned East and penned his reminiscences of Plains life. And it was this court-martial which made him so eager to distinguish himself a year later when called back into service. It was this eagerness for military glory at the expense of the Plains Indians which became the impelling factor behind his vicious Washita campaign, his first major assignment upon lifting of the court-martial sentence in the autumn of 1868.

CHAPTER FOUR

The Last "Scrap of Paper"

*H*ANCOCK'S vaunted expedition a complete failure, Custer baffled and disgraced, the whole frontier again ablaze with retaliatory raids from the Black Hills to the Arkansas, peace advocates finally made themselves heard. Millions of dollars had been spent, hundreds of lives of soldiers, settlers and freighters had been sacrificed, yet the Indians were complete masters of the situation.

Further, despite efforts of the military to keep the nation incited by misleading stories of Indian depredations, the populace was beginning to sympathize largely with the red man. Washington became convinced the situation could be adjusted more quickly and more economically as well as more honorably by diplomacy than by force of arms.

At the same time, the Government found the Indians less willing to risk their newly regained freedom on documents which became "mere scraps of paper" whenever designing white men believed themselves able to tear up these treaties with impunity. They had been double-crossed too often to be rushed into new pacts.

During the decade immediately preceding the Battle of the Washita, around which this narrative is woven, constant excuse for military operations against these Plains Indians was to "make the savages live up to their treaty obligations." Exhauustive search has been made for authentication of a single instance in which any of those Indians against which the Washita Expedition was to be directed ever violated any treaty with the white man until white man's repeated aggressions, in contravention of these obligations, incited Indian reprisals.[1] On the contrary, General W. S. Harney, who headed the military group when the famous Medicine Lodge Peace Treaty was negotiated, once said:

> I never knew an Indian chief to break his word . . . I have lived on this frontier fifty years and I have never yet known an instance in which war broke out with these tribes that the tribes were not in the right.

So far as Black Kettle's Cheyennes were concerned, as well as those involved in the Hancock-Custer campaign of 1867, no effort at making a territorial treaty with them is of record until about the time of the outbreak of the Civil War. At that time, William W. Bent was agent for the non-reservation Indians south of the Arkansas. Years of harassment by the soldiers had worried their leaders into seeking an amicable agreement over lands so that the Indians might hunt without molestation. Some were so eager for a cessation of hostilities, always incited by troops, that they were even willing to try their hands at agriculture. The great majority, however, preferred to continue their lives as roving huntsmen yet within such reasonable restrictions as would prevent collision with settlers and soldiers. They appealed to Bent to try to arrange such a treaty council for them.

He did so. Cheyennes and Arapahoes persuaded the Comanches to join. An effort was made to bring in the Kiowas, too, but the Kiowas, at that time, were enjoying one of their sporadic wars against the Utes, so they refused. The other tribes, however, met a commission at Bent's Fort, south and east of Denver not far from where the Sand Creek massacre was to occur a few years later. There they entered into extended negotiations.

No definite agreement could be reached at that

1. See Appendix B.

time. The commissioners wanted to exclude the Indians from the Republican and Smoky Hill regions. These were favorite hunting grounds of the Cheyennes and Arapahoes. The region the commissioners wanted the Indians to accept as their reservation had been virtually cleared of buffalo. Agriculture could be successfully accomplished only through irrigation. The council finally broke up without signatures of the Indians to these terms.

Particularly adamant in their refusals to cede the Republican and Smoky Hill hunting grounds were all the Dog Soldier chiefs. Not one of them would put his mark to the treaty offered them. In this connection it should be remembered it was a Dog Soldier village in this very region. with a few Sioux attached to it, that Custer and Hancock were to sack to precipitate the Indian war of 1867.

Later, however, Agent Boone rallied some of these chiefs who had participated in the Bent's Fort conference and obtained their signatures. Within three years, military expeditions violated this pact. Soldier aggressions culminated in the Sand Creek massacre and resultant raids of reprisal.

Other attempts were made in the years immediately following the first abortive treaty, but all came to naught until 1865. Always, with new treaties apparently in sight, soldiers then in service in that region would be guilty of killing friendly Indians. This, under the red man's code, demanded reprisals. Such acts engendered distrust as well. Most momentous of such treacherous acts was the Sand Creek massacre of November 29, 1864. It required nearly a year following this attack to quiet the Indians to a point where they were willing to enter into treaty negotiations once more.

Black Kettle finally brought this about. Cheyennes, Arapahoes, Kiowas and Comanches participated. A point on the little Arkansas about eight miles above its mouth was agreed upon as the council ground. Black Kettle was the first Indian chief to sign the resultant treaty. Dog Soldier chiefs, such as Tall Bull, Bull Bear, and White Horse, those encountered by Custer and Hancock eighteen months later on Pawnee Fork, again refused to sign the pact because the agreement called for relinquisment of their claim to the Smoky Hill hunting grounds. Nor would they yield when again contacted the following year and importuned to join the signatories. This was one year before the Hancock-Custer expedition.

That expedition now had scrapped this treaty, too.

The little Arkansas pact had provided, among other things:

> that hereafter perpetual peace shall be maintained between the people and the Government of the United States and the Indians, parties hereto . . . And the Indians, parties hereto, on their part agree, in case crimes or other violations of law shall be committed by any persons, members of their tribe, such person or persons shall, upon complaint being made, in writing, to their agent, Superintendent of Indian Affairs. or other proper authority, by the party injured, and verified by affidavit, be delivered to the person duly authorized to take such person or persons into custody, to the end that such person or persons may be punished according to the laws of the United States.

Further, the section from which the above is quoted states specifically:

> such hostile acts or depredations shall not be redressed by force or arms.

Yet Custer and Hancock had started a war without any legitimate cause whatsoever. Kiowas, it is true, had seized white prisoners. But the Government did not follow provisions of the treaty applicable to such an act. It did not demand the tribe involved surrender the guilty to be punished under the laws of the United States. Instead, General Hancock, at the head of a military force, had attempted to "obtain redress by force of arms." He had sought redress, not from the guilty Kiowas, but from the peaceable Indians hundreds of miles distant from the region where the act complained of was perpetrated. He having done so, it was with the greatest of difficulty those opposed to military domination of the Plains could induce the red man to retire from the warpath and consent to talk peace again.

Other breaches of the treaty of 1865 by the Whites further tended to destroy faith of the Indians in the Great White Father's promises. They made Indian leaders hesitant about attempting to commit their followers again. Black Kettle, Seven Bulls, Little Robe, and Black White Man, Cheyenne chiefs who had escaped the Sand Creek massacre yet had all their property destroyed by Chivington's men, had been promised three hundred and twenty acres, each of his own choosing, as reparation for their losses at that time. Each Indian woman widowed, or any Indian child deprived of a parent during that raid, was promised choice of one hundred sixty acres of land. All were promised reimbursement for possessions lost on that occasion.

Eighteen months had gone by without these pledges being fulfilled by the Government. The Government, too, had promised each Indian of the signatory tribes subsistence and goods to the amount of twenty dollars each year. These promised articles had not been delivered.

While this agreement had established limits of permanent reservations for the southern tribes in territory south of the Kansas line, it specifically stipulated "that until the Indians parties hereto have removed to the reservation provided for . . . . . they hereby are expressly permitted to reside upon and range at pleasure throughout the unsettled portions of that part of the country they claim as originally theirs, which lies between the Arkansas and the Platte rivers."

Yet Hancock and Custer had attacked them in that very unsettled region.

Thus, when Custer had been sent into exile through court-martial, and troops had been withdrawn from the field, the Government knew it would have great difficulty bringing Indians into conference again for one more attempt at diplomatically settling for all time, their controversies. Furthermore, the Government desired to establish similar agreements with every tribe and every band on the Plains, from Canada to Red River. These included the Cheyennes, Arapahoes, and Sioux of the North as well as the Cheyennes, Arapahoes, Kiowas, Comanches and Apaches of the South.

First concern were the southern tribesmen. Responsibility for contacting these bands and making arrangements for a peace conference fell largely upon the shoulders of Agents J. H. Leavenworth and E. W. Wynkoop. Their ministrations to these tribes had been so faithful over a comparatively long period of time that even their failure to stop the Hancock-Custer expedition had not shaken faith of the Indians in their proven friends. But their wards now were scattered all over the southern prairies, from the Arkansas and its northern tributaries to Red River. They were broken up into comparatively small bands for the summer with little prospect of reuniting into large villages before winter. But the Government did not want to wait until winter to launch this new treaty effort.

Agent Leavenworth first called upon George Bent, a half-blood Cheyenne. Runners found Bent with a band of Cheyennes on the Sweetwater, north and west of the Wichita Mountains. The agent asked Bent to bring some of the most important chiefs for a conference near where the Little Arkan-

sas pact of two years before had been executed.
Bent, in turn, turned to Black Kettle. Though Black
Kettle had been deposed as head of his nation soon
after his reliance in the white man's word had resulted in the slaughter of many of his people on
Sand Creek, he gradually had regained his prestige
and once more Bent knew him to be the most powerful peace advocate among all the southern no-
mads. Bent knew it was to keep his people out of
the Western Kansas trouble that Black Kettle had
withdrawn far south of the Kansas line.

At first Black Kettle protested it was useless,
at that time, to attempt to bring his followers into
further negotiations with the Government. He pointed out that killing of two of his men by Hancock's
scouts near the Pawnee Fork village had fanned
smoldering fires of resentment among all the Cheyennes. Eventually, however, he agreed to make one
more effort.

Taking only a few leaders with them, Black Kettle and Bent met Agent Leavenworth at the place
appointed. There they were joined by representatives of the Kiowas, Comanches, Arapahoes and
Apaches. Advised that the Government desired to
make a lasting peace with all Indians and would
send a great quantity of supplies to them, the chiefs
were asked to suggest the most suitable location
for such a conference. Since supplies were to be
sent from Fort Larned, Agent Leavenworth recommended that some spot be selected as near that
post as possible in order to make it easy to get proposed presents to those who should attend.

Black Kettle wanted to confer with his people
before making any definite selection of a council
point. So did some of the others. Black Eagle, a
Kiowa, said there was an old Kiowa medicine lodge
on a stream known as Medicine Lodge Creek not
far from the Kansas line and not far from Fort

Larned. There was to be found water and timber and suitable ground for pitching the various camps. Further, wagon trains bearing supplies would find no obstacles between Fort Larned and this location. It was agreed that all should endeavor to prevail upon their associates to accept this place.

Followed days of feverish activity in contacting the various bands scattered throughout the region south of the Arkansas and arranging for the headmen to go to Fort Larned to make preliminary arrangements with Agent Leavenworth. Upon arriving at Fort Larned, they found not only Agent Leavenworth waiting to talk with them, but Thomas Murphy, Superintendent of Indian Affairs, as well.

Medicine Lodge Creek having been agreed upon as the council place, several weeks were spent freighting immense stores to that spot, the superintendent directing all arrangements.

Gradually the Indians assembled. Some had come north with their leaders at the time of the preliminary councils with Agent Leavenworth and Superintendent Murphy. These went into camp within a few hours' ride of the council place. Others joined them from time to time.

By the first of October nearly every band of any consequence on the Southern Plains was represented either by its entire membership or, at least, by its headmen and chiefs. A few Comanches and one large contingent of Cheyennes were the only absentees at that time. Their tardiness delayed the main conference several days. It took repeated efforts on the part of Black Kettle finally to bring in the recalcitrant Cheyennes after two weeks urging. They had been afraid to trust the word of the white man again, they said, in explaining this hesitancy. Missing Comanches also came in.

During this delay, many informal conferences were held between commissioners and various bands in order to ascertain in advance of the formal conference, the views of the Indians on the important subjects to be debated.

When finally convened, this Medicine Lodge peace council developed into one of the most pretentious and most momentous parleys between the so-called "barbarians" and representatives of white civilization in history.[2]

Heading the commission authorized by Congress to negotiate this treaty was Nathaniel G. Taylor of Tennessee, its president. General W. S. Harney was the senior army officer designated to represent the Government. He had been among the Plains Indians longer than any other officer present. He understood them and their problem as a result of this extended contact. Although a representative of the military branch of the government, his sympathies were with the red men. General Sherman also had been appointed a member of the commission. He had been with it a few weeks previously when it had conferred with a few of the Sioux

2. The whole story of the Indian wars from 1868 on revolves around the Medicine Lodge peace pact negotiated on Medicine Lodge Creek, Kansas, in October, 1867. While only the Southern "wild tribes" were represented, their knowledge of conditions and desires of Plains Indians was so comprehensive and their mastery of diplomacy and argument so keen that they were able to prepare a pact agreeable to those of the Northern Plains as well, Sioux, Northern Cheyennes and Northern Arapahoes.

This accomplishment stamps Black Kettle, Little Raven, Satanta and their contemporaries as masters of diplomacy, evidence of intellects in this respect comparable with the greatest white diplomats of that era.

Although all subsequent Plains Indian wars were the direct or indirect result of disputes arising from contradictory interpretations of the terms of this treaty, the text of this pact never has been reproduced in any of the many books dealing with events of this period, except official documents. Since these may not be readily available to all readers of this narrative, the full text and signatures are presented herein as Appendix C.

A study of the signatures is worth while, for many of those signing were to play leading roles in subsequent wars.

at North Platte, Nebraska, but had been recalled and General C. C. Augur had been named in his place. Other representatives of the Great Father were General Alfred H. Terry, J. B. Sanborn, Colonel Samuel F. Tappan and United States, Senator J. B. Henderson.

Participating in advisory capacities were Thomas Murphy, superintendent; Colonel Leavenworth, and Major Wynkoop, tribal agents; John D. Howland, clerk of the commission as well as a newspaper representative; A. S. White, secretary, and Alfred A. Taylor, assistant secretary; Governor S. J. Crawford; Lieutenant Governor Root, and Senator E. G. Ross of Kansas; James A. Hardy, inspector general of the United States army; Samuel S. Smoot, United States surveyor; James Taylor, artist; George B. Willis, phonographer and a number of interpreters including Philip McCusker, John Smith, George Bent and C. W. Whittaker.

Escorting troops were commanded by Major Joel H. Elliott, Seventh Cavalry, later to be sacrificed to these same Indians by Custer. This force consisted of two companies of the Seventh Cavalry with four mountain howitzers.

Newspapers were represented by such notables as Henry M. Stanley of the New York Tribune, James E. Taylor of Frank Leslie's, Jack Howland of Harper's Weekly and others.

More Cheyennes than Indians of any other tribes were there. They were represented in the eventual signing of the pact by Bull Bear, famous Dog Soldier chief, Tall Bull and White Horse of the same society; Black Kettle, Spotted Elk, Buffalo Calf, Slim Face, Gray Head, Little Rock, Curley Hair, Little Robe, Whirlwind, and Heap of Birds.

Next in order of numbers were the Arapahoes represented by Little Raven, Yellow Bear, Storm, White Rabbit, Spotted Wolf, Little Big Mouth, Young Colt and Tall Bear.

Speaking for the Kiowas were Satank, Satanta, Black Eagle, Kicking Eagle, Stinking Saddle Cloth, Woman's Heart, Stumbling Bear, One Bear, The Crow and Bear Lying Down.

Representing the Comanches were Ten Bears, Painted Lips, Silver Breech, Standing Feather, Gap in the Woods, Horseback, Wolf's Name, Little Horn, Dog Fat, Iron Mountain.

It was early in October when the commissioners first arrived. It was more than two weeks later before they finally had adjusted matters sufficiently to settle down to actual preparation of the treaties. It was October 28 before these pacts finally were completed and signed.

Indian spokesmen proved as effective in argument and treaty making as their astute contemporaries. Black Kettle of the Cheyennes, Little Raven of the Arapahoes and Satanta of the Kiowas were their chief spokesmen. Particularly effective was Little Raven. It was chiefly through his dramatic presentation of the wrongs done the Indians that a section was written into the original pact providing for payment of all back annuities and for restitution and damages for losses sustained by the Cheyennes and Arapahoes in the Sand Creek massacre.

Without ever advising the Indians of the change, however, this entire article was stricken by Congress when the document came up for ratification months later.

But so far as the actual writing of the treaty was concerned, the red men scored a diplomatic triumph.

The document commenced by stipulating that

From this day forward, all war between the parties of this agreement shall forever cease. The Government of the United States desires peace, and its honor is here pledged to keep it. The Indians desire peace, and they now pledge their honor to keep it.

Continuing, the next paragraph read:

> If bad men among the whites, or among other people
> subject to the authority of the United States, shall
> commit any wrong upon the person or property of the
> Indians, the United States, will upon proof made to
> the agent and forwarded to the Commissioner of In-
> dian Affairs at Washington City, proceed at once to
> cause the offender to be arrested and punished ac-
> cording to the laws of the United States, and also
> reimburse the injured person for the loss sustained.

Here was what the Indians wanted more than
anything else—assurance of peace and freedom from
aggression by the bad white men who heretofore had
caused so much resentment among the red men.

Thus assured, the Indians were willing to make
the same kind of promises to the Whites. They
agreed to deliver up any of their own people who
should stray from the straight and narrow and to
permit the Government to withhold any of their mon-
ies to pay for any legitimate claims of damage done
by their people.

They obtained for their reservations and hunting
grounds most of the territory from the southern line
of the State of Kansas to Red River not reserved
for other tribes. In the words of the treaty, this
territory was

> hereby set apart for the absolute and undisturbed use
> and occupation of the Indians herein named, and for
> such other friendly tribes or individual Indians   as
> from time to time they may be willing, with the con-
> sent of the United States, to admit among them; and
> the United States now solemnly agrees that no per-
> son except such officers and agents, and employees
> of the government as may be authorized to enter
> upon Indian reservations in discharge of their duties
> enjoined by law, shall ever be permitted to pass over,
> settle upon, or reside in the territory described in this
> article, or in such territory as may be added to this
> reservation for use of said Indians.

As will be noted later, it was trouble growing out
of invasion of these lands by alien Kaws, wards of
the Government, and renegade Whites residing in

the vicinity of Council Grove, Kansas, which eventually resulted in organization of the Sheridan-Custer campaign of 1868. It is typical of frontier injustice of those days that though the Cheyennes, Arapahoes, Kiowas and Comanches were the ones against whose treaty rights these offenders operated, yet it was the Cheyennes, Arapahoes, Kiowas and Comanches who were punished by the Government.

They obtained promise of the Government to construct at some place near the center of these reservations, permanent agency buildings. These buildings were to include a warehouse for the use of the agents in storing goods belonging to the Indians, an agency building for the use of the agent, residences for the carpenter, farmer, blacksmith, miller and engineer and school buildings as well as a sawmill, grist mill and shingle mill.

There were to be separate reservations for the Cheyennes and Arapahoes, and for the Kiowas, Comanches, and Apaches. Cheyenne and Arapahoe lands were established in the northern portion of this area, Kiowa and Comanche and Apache lands in the south. Each of these groups was to have its own central agency and agency buildings.

They obtained promise of individual allotments for any who desired to try their hands at agriculture, and services of competent instructors and necessary implements.

They obtained promise of annual issuance of clothing and subsistence.

They obtained the right to hunt unmolested on any of the land south of the Arkansas so long as the buffalo should range thereon in such numbers as to justify the chase.

In return they agreed that they would withdraw all opposition to construction of the railroad then being built through the Smoky Hill region; that they would permit the peaceable construction of any railroad not passing over their reservation; that they would not attack any white person at home or traveling; they would not carry off from the settlements white women or children; that they would not harm white men not encroaching on the Indian's rights; that they would permit roads or railroads to be built through their reservations if the government should pay damages; and that no treaty in the future would be binding unless signed by three-fourths of all the adult male Indians occupying the land involved or interested in it.

Identical treaties were signed with the Cheyennes and the Arapahoes and with the other three southern tribes, except for certain necessary differences as to boundaries of their respective reservations.

They were satisfied bands of red men which quit the council grounds to return to their promised land. It was a gratified commission which departed soon thereafter to complete negotiations with the Sioux, the Northern Cheyennes, the Northern Arapahoes and the Utes.

By agreement, the Utes went to Washington to complete their treaty. Pacts with the various divisions of the Sioux nation were made near the close of the winter. So was that with the Northern Cheyennes and Northern Arapahoes who were given their choice of establishing their reservations in the lands set aside for the Sioux in the North, or with their kinsmen, the Cheyennes and Arapahoes of the South.

The Medicine Lodge treaty was the crowning diplomatic effort for the pacification of the Plains.

But like all previous treaties, it soon was to become a mere "scrap of paper"—the last "scrap of paper" so far as the Southern Plains Indians were concerned.

CHAPTER FIVE

Organizing the Washita Campaign

$\mathcal{G}$OVERNMENT machinery always did move slowly, most exasperatingly so. Consequently it was not until late summer of the next year, 1868, that the Medicine Lodge treaty finally was amended by Congress, ratified and promulgated.

Meantime, the military forces were not content to let well enough alone. On the contrary, many of their acts aggravated the Indians. Nor could the red man understand why the Great White Father was so slow about providing for them, as he had promised to do. He seemed to expect them to move on to their reservations immediately, although no steps had been taken to care for them there, in accordance with terms of their agreement. He apparently was making no appreciable effort to provide them with the things he had promised them, so that they could begin to "travel the white man's road."[1]

While pacific agencies in the East were striving to aid Indian agents of the West in getting the Government to ratify the treaties and carry out its part of the contract expeditiously and faithfully, military leaders still on the Plains were invoking every pretext to move against the Indians throughout the summer. They were even planning a tremendous winter campaign in direct conflict with the letter as well as the spirit of the treaties.

General Sheridan took command of the Division of the Missouri in March. He established field head-

1. See Appendix D.

quarters at Fort Larned, most important military post in that region. This was four months after execution of the Medicine Lodge pact. Not understanding the red tape through which such affairs had to pass to become "official" and effective, the Indians sent word they wanted to talk to Sheridan about these things. They not only wanted to know why the Government had failed to send them the things it had promised them but also they desired to consult with him about the boundaries of their reservations. Some said they did not know just how far their legal hunting grounds, reserved for them under the pact, extended. Some said the Government's understanding of these boundaries was not the same as that of the Indians.

Sheridan refused to grant them audience. Instead, he moved his headquarters to Fort Dodge where he would not be so close to them. Thus he would avoid the annoyance of repeated efforts of the chiefs to confer with him.

Such evasions naturally increased the rapidly mounting discontent of the tribes. Then, too, it was no uncommon thing for the Kaws and some of their affiliated mixed-bloods, as well as venturesome Whites, to aggravate the situation by intruding upon lands the so-called wild tribes considered their exclusive domain.

Council Grove, as the seat of the Kaw Agency, was a storm center. It was also the last trading post on the Santa Fe trail and was regarded as the most remote frontier white settlement. It marked the westernmost outpost of civilization in what was then Western Kansas. Here that spring occurred an incident which was destined to become the indirect predicate for the Washita campaign.[2]

Provoked by actions of the Kaws in invading

2. See Appendix E.

their hunting grounds, the Cheyennes and Arapahoes sent word that, if these tresspassers did not behave themselves, reprisals would be launched. Straightway the Kaws, fearing for the consequences to themselves, should their enemies decide to attack, sent word to Agent Boone that the Cheyennes were planning to raid that region. Agent Boone went to investigate. He was accompanied by Major Stover.

While Agent Boone and Major Stover were talking to the Kaws, a band of Cheyennes dashed by in one of those wild demonstrations all Plains Indians were accustomed to stage on such occasions. Pretending to believe their enemies were attacking, the Kaws sent a fusillade after them. The Cheyennes made no effort to respond in like manner to this unexpectedly hostile reception. They halted at a safe distance and sent in a messenger to say they had learned of the agent's arrival and had come to have a talk with him.

Taking Major Stover with him, Agent Boone went to talk to the Cheyennes, who had withdrawn to a hillside. There the chiefs suggested that two Cheyennes and two Kaws lay aside their arms and meet between the lines with the agent and major to adjust difficulties which had arisen. At that very instant the Kaws charged past, firing at the group on the hillside. None was hit although bullets whistled close to the agent and major and assembled Cheyennes.

This challenge was more than the patience of the Cheyennes could endure. Leading their white guests to a point of safety, they engaged the Kaws in a battle lasting several hours. Finally the Cheyennes rode off to their camp on Diamond Creek, after telling Boone they would await there the pleasure of the Kaws—war or peace. On the way, they dashed through the settlement, fired two buildings belonging to half-breeds and robbing three citizen farmers.

Not long thereafter Little Robe brought back a band of more than one hundred Cheyennes to the vicinity of Council Grove. During this visit they took seven head of cattle belonging to ranchers but later told the agent at Fort Larned they would make restitution if they could find out to whom these cattle had belonged. They said they had taken these beeves because they needed food. They also begged four steers from a trail herd being driven across their reservation from Texas to the Kansas markets.

The story of these incidents sounded very much different when it reached higher government officials. Embellished, it placed the Cheyennes in the role of marauding hostiles. Forthwith came an order from the Superintendent of Indian Affairs at Washington to Agent Wynkoop instructing him to withhold arms and ammunition promised Cheyennes under the Medicine Lodge treaty. This was in June.[3]

In July, Cheyennes, Arapahoes and Apaches went to Fort Larned for their issues. Arapahoes and Apaches were given their food and clothing supplies. Promised arms and ammunition were held back several days. The Cheyennes were told they could have other issues but no guns or powder or lead or caps; that the Great White Father was displeased with them because they had raided around Council Grove, hence he did not propose to place in their hands any implements of warfare.

It was an amazed group of chieftains who received this information. "Had not the Kaws picked the quarrel?" they asked. The agent was there when the trouble occurred and saw this with his own eyes. Surely there must be some mistake. Supplies sent them by the Government were inadequate. Their families would be hungry when winter came unless the warriors could kill buffalo. They could not kill

3. See Appendix F.

GENERAL PHILIP H. SHERIDAN

buffalo without guns and without ammunition. The agent knew, too, they insisted, that the white settlers had encroached upon the Indians' land and had fired on Indians more than once recently, yet the Cheyennes had not retaliated. Was this any way to treat them? Certainly they had done nothing since the treaty was signed warranting punishment of the entire tribe.

Said Black Kettle:

"Our white brothers are pulling away from us the hand they gave us at Medicine Lodge; but we will try to hold on to it. We hope the Great White Father will take pity on us and let us have the guns and ammunition he promised us so we can go hunt buffalo to keep our families from going hungry."

Critical though their situation was, the Cheyennes refused to accept other issues pending adjustment of the dispute over guns and ammunition promised them for hunting purposes.

In Agent Wynkoop, they found a sympathetic mediator. He knew the Cheyennes were justified in their position. He appreciated the patience with which they had received such disappointing news. At the same time, he secretly doubted ability of the chiefs and older men to hold in leash indefinitely the fretting young warriors. He knew the young hot bloods would be eager to go on the warpath, now that the Great White Father had broken faith with them. Therefore, late in July, the agent sent an urgent message to the Interior Department, requesting permission to turn over to the Cheyennes all the goods on hand that belonged to them.

He wrote:

> UPPER ARKANSAS AGENCY,
> FORT LARNED, KANSAS
> July 20, 1868.
>
> Sir:
>
> I have the honor to report that I have issued the annuity goods to the Arapahoes and Apaches of my

agency, but, when the Cheyennes found that they were not to receive their arms and ammunition, they desired me to retain their goods until the government saw fit to let them have their guns and ammunition. I have, therefore, their goods stored at my post. They felt much disappointed, but gave no evidence of being angry, but on the contrary expressed themselves to the effect that, although they thought their white brothers were pulling away from them the hand they had given them at Medicine Lodge Creek, nevertheless they would try to hold on to it and would wait with patience for the Great White Father to take pity on them and let them have the arms and ammunition which had been promised them and which they considered they had not forfeited by any direct violation of any treaty pledges such as would affect the whole nation; they referred to numerous incidents of which I was cognizant of their having been treated badly by the whites since the treaty, been fired upon, etc., in no instance of which they had retaliated.

I cannot too strongly urge upon the department the policy of issuing the arms and ammunition as soon as possible, and am in hopes daily of receiving an order to that effect.

I have the honor to be, with much respect, your obedient servant.

E. W. WYNKOOP,
U. S. Indian Agent

Hon. Thos Murphy,
Superintendent of Indian Affairs.

Also in sympathy with the Cheyennes were other Plains tribes, particularly their closest allies, the Arapahoes. From every section came grumbling that rapidly grew into an ominous rumble.

The furore in Kansas was echoed farther south. There a similar situation had developed, involving Kiowas and Comanches. Having made peace with the white man in the north, Satanta and some of his contemporaries had gone into Texas to make peace with the Whites there. They did not know, at that time, that Texas was a part of the United States. Their overtures had been received with hostilities.

They had been fired upon. They had retaliated by seizing white hostages. For this, all of their annuities had been denied them.

Fearing a general uprising might result, the Commissioner of Indian Affairs in Washington instructed Superintendent Murphy to issue supplies and guns to the Cheyennes if convinced that such action was necessary to prevent war breaking out. Commissioner Taylor telegraphed from Washington:

> DEPARTMENT OF THE INTERIOR,
> OFFICE OF INDIAN AFFAIRS,
> Washington, D. C., July 23, 1868
>
> The Secretary of the Interior directs that you exercise your discretion about issuing to the Indians all their annuity goods, including their arms and ammunition which were promised and provided.
>
> If you are satisfied that the issue of the arms and ammunition is necessary to preserve the peace and that no evil will result from their delivery, let the Indians have them.
>
> Superintendent Murphy leaves this evening for Fort Larned.
>
> N. G. TAYLOR, Commissioner.
>
> E. W. Wynkoop, Esq.,
> United States Indian Agent, Fort Larned.

Not until August was this done.

That was a few days too late. Believing the Government had repudiated its agreement, a band of Cheyennes and Arapahoes, which had been encamped on Walnut Creek, decided to make war on their old enemies, the Pawnees. On the way north they found buffalo scarce. As they neared the settlements of the Saline Valley, a small group went in to get something to eat. Included among the foragers was a brother of White Antelope, martyred chief of Sand Creek, and Red Nose.

White Antelope's brother never had forgiven the Whites for their atrocious Sand Creek massacre. When this opportunity for revenge presented itself, he could not resist the temptation to attack a white woman and carry her away. In this, Red Nose was an accomplice. When these miscreants rejoined the main band, the others reproached them for these acts. They returned the white woman to her people.

Then the band resumed its journey northward, toward the land of the Pawnees, little knowing that serious trouble was just around the corner.

It so happened this incident occurred about the same time the belated issuance of annuities, including guns and ammunition, was being made to the Cheyennes. While not a single one of those in this war party had received any of the goods or guns thus issued, nor even had knowledge that the issue was to be made, the militarists in Washington argued that this raid was conclusive evidence that the Indians were acting in bad faith. Propagandists said that the instant the Cheyennes came into possession of guns and ammunition they immediately started depredating. The march of this single band against the Pawnees was heralded as a general frontier uprising.[4]

Meanwhile Agent Wynkoop, learning of the Saline incident, sent for Little Rock, one of the principal chief of the Cheyennes. In keeping with provisions of the Medicine Lodge treaty, the agent determined to ask those in authority amongst the Indians to search out the guilty and deliver them for trial. This Little Rock agreed to do.

Six days later he reported the band which had gone to hunt the Pawnees included such Cheyenne personages as Tall Wolf, son of Medicine Arrow, Porcupine Bear, son of Big Head, Bear that Goes Ahead;

---

4. The Cheyenne war party left the camp of the remainder of their tribesmen above the forks of Walnut Creek to go against the Pawnees, August 2. The issue of arms to the others did not take place until August 9. Report of Indian Affairs, 1868, pages 70-72.

Red Nose and a brother of White Antelope. Among the Arapahoes was a son of Little Raven, head chief of the Arapahoes.

It was White Antelope's brother and Red Nose who had ravished the white woman. Inasmuch as the others had protested this act and had forced them to return her to her own people, Little Rock argued that only these two should be surrendered.

Wynkoop disagreed. He demanded delivery of all those named.

While protesting that he doubted the tribes would yield all of them, Little Rock agreed to do his best to bring about their surrender. Should he be unsuccessful, he asked permission to bring his own family to the agency, for he realized a conflict likely would result.

But in the trouble zone events were moving with a rapidity which prevented peaceable settlement of the matter. No sooner had the marauding band returned its woman captive to her people and had resumed its journey toward the land of the Pawnees than it encountered soldiers and vigilantes. Fighting resulted. Believing the Whites had declared war, this band began promiscuous raiding.

News of the fighting spread to Whites and Indians alike. Other bands went on the warpath. From August through October the conflict raged along the Saline, Solomon and Republican rivers. There also were outbreaks in Texas and Colorado. Stage coaches and wagon trains were attacked. Ranches were raided and burned. More than one hundred Whites were killed, exclusive of losses in military engagements. Hundreds of horses, mules and cattle were driven off. Official records show that less than a dozen Indians were slain during all this trouble.

Only a miracle prevented an entire detachment of fifty scouts under Colonel George A. Forsythe being annihilated when they picked a fight with a large band of Cheyennes and Sioux on the Arickaree Fork of the Republican River.[5]

And farther south, General Alfred Sully, leading several companies of the Seventh Cavalry, supported by detachments from the Third Infantry, set forth to drive all hostiles in Southern Kansas across the state line into what is now Western Oklahoma.

Unable to overtake any of the roving bands in Kansas, Sully followed their trails on south. He finally encountered them along the Cimarron River. Followed two days of sporadic fighting in which the troops were complete worsted. They lost one man captured, a second wounded, and a third killed.

Sully turned back after reaching the sand hills of Beaver Creek. The Indians followed, harassing his flanks and rear until he had been driven from that region. Soon they followed him to his camp on Bluff Creek in Southern Kansas where they continued to torment and taunt the soldiers who did not dare to leave camp any distance for fear of being killed or captured by their ever alert besiegers.

Smarting under criticism from those who believed the Indians were being grossly mistreated, yet determined to make the most of this opportunity to crush the red men of the Southern Plains, General Sherman and General Sheridan speeded preparations for the proposed winter campaign. They determined to make it a bruising campaign, a campaign of annihilation if necessary—or if excusable.

Three expeditions were planned.

The main drive was to be pointed directly south from Fort Dodge, its ultimate destination being the Wichita Mountains. Everything from the Arkansas to the Wichitas was to be subdued. This punitive expedition was to be under direct command of Gen-

5. See Appendix G.

COLONEL SAMUEL J. CRAWFORD

Pictured in the uniform he wore in the
Washita Campaign.

eral Sheridan. It was to consist of a regiment of Kansas volunteers, recruited especially for this campaign, in addition to the Seventh Cavalry, regulars, and Forsyth's scouts.[6]

Another column under Colonel A. W. Evans was to move east from Fort Bascom, New Mexico. It was to consist of six companies of cavalry and three companies of infantry, accompanied by a supply train. It was to be pointed across the Staked Plains to the Wichitas to turn back any bands which might try to escape in that direction when Sheridan's command moved down from the north.

A third was to be in command of General Eugene A. Carr, then stationed in the former haunts of the Indians of the upper Arkansas who once roamed in Colorado. General Carr, with his seven troops of cavalry was to outfit and start from Fort Lyon. All three of these columns were to converge on the area between the Antelope Hills on the Canadian River and the Wichita Mountains.

General Carr's march was uneventful. That of Colonel Evans encountered one band just west of the Wichitas on Christmas day. A surprise attack resulted in few casualites. General Carr did not pass the Antelope Hills.

It was to be a different story for the more pretentious expedition to be mobilized on the Arkansas.

To aid here, General Sheridan wanted a leader for the Seventh Cavalry more fitted for the arduous task confronting it than the aged Sully. General Custer was the man he desired for this assignment but Custer still was in Monroe finishing the suspension imposed upon him by court-martial.

Generals Sheridan and Sherman conferred. They decided to appeal to Washington for a lifting of the sentence. They did not know just how long it would

6. See Appendix H.

take officials in the national capital to act, but they hoped Washington would be more expeditious in this matter than it had been in taking care of Government obligations to the Indians. Sheridan sent a telegram to Washington. Then he wired **General** Custer in his northern retreat:

> HEADQUARTERS DEPARTMENT OF THE MISSOURI IN THE FIELD, FORT HAYS, KANSAS, Sept. 28, 1868.
> GENERAL G. A. CUSTER, Monroe, Michigan:
> General Sherman, Sully and myself, and nearly all of the officers of your regiment have asked for you, and I hope the application will be successful. Can you come at once? Eleven companies of your regiment will move about the 1st of October against the hostile Indians, from Medicine Lodge Creek toward the Wichita Mountains.
> (Signed) P. H. SHERIDAN, Major General
> Commanding

Could he come at once? Could he? Would he? Here was balm for wounded pride. Here was opportunity to erase the stigma of his court-martial. He had considered himself the official "goat" for failure of the Hancock Expedition. That expedition had cost the nation millions of dollars and more than three hundred lives, yet it had been a flop so far as punishing the Indians was concerned. Somebody had to take a rap for it and Custer still was rankled that that somebody had been he. The wild red men had been responsible for his abject humiliation. Now he would even the score. Just let him at them! They never would outwit him again. All rules of civilized warfare would be suspended, so far as he was concerned.

Without waiting for Washington's confirmation of his return to active service, General Custer, accompanied by his wife, was on his way to the frontier within forty-eight hours. Notice of lifting of his court-martial sentence reached him before he reached Fort Hays, terminus of the Kansas-Pacific railway at that time. With ill-concealed impatience, he departed Fort Hays. There he left his wife. He went by way of Fort Leavenworth to Fort Dodge, near which post his command was operating. He found it on Bluff Creek.

His men hailed Custer's return with rejoicing. They, too, had new scores to settle with the Indians to the south, some more recently acquired than Custer's humiliation.

Even then they were being harassed by those Indians which had followed Sully's command all the way from Beaver Creek.

Within a few hours after Custer had rejoined the Seventh, the Indians made one of their typical attacks. Custer described it thus:

> I was in the act of taking my seat for dinner, my ride having given me a splendid relish for the repast, when the shouts and firing of the savages informed me that more serious duties were at hand.
>
> Every man flew to arms and almost without command rushed to oppose the enemy. Officers and men provided themselves with rifles or carbines and soon began delivering a deliberate but ineffective fire against the Indians. The latter, as usual, were merely practicing their ordinary ruse de guerre, which was to display a very small venturesome force and, after having led the pursuing force well away from the main body, to surround and destroy it by the aid of overwhelming numbers previously concealed in a ravine or ambush until the proper moment.
>
> On this occasion the stratagem did not succeed. The Indians, being mounted on their fleetest ponies, would charge in single file past our camp, often riding within easy carbine range of our men, displaying great boldness and unsurpassed horsemanship. The soldiers, unaccustomed to firing at such rapidly moving objects, were rarely able to inflict serious damage upon their enemies. Occasionally a pony would be struck and brought to the ground, but the rider always succeeded in being carried away upon the pony of a comrade.
>
> It was interesting to witness their marvelous abilities

as horsemen, at the same time one could not but admire the courage they displayed. The ground was level, open and unobstructed; the troops were formed in an irregular line of skirmish dismounted, the line extending a distance of perhaps two hundred yards. The Indians had a rendezvous behind a hillock on the right, which prevented them from being seen or disturbed by the soldiers. Starting out singly, or by twos and threes, the warriors would suddenly leave the cover of the hillock and with war whoops dash over the plain in a line parallel to that occupied by the soldiers and within easy carbine range of the latter. The pony seemed possessed of the designs and wishes of his dusky rider, as he seemed to fly unguided by bridle, rein or spur. The warrior would fire and load and fire again as often as he was able to, while dashing along through the shower of leaden bullets fired above, beneath, in front and behind him by the excited troopers, until finally, when the aim of the latter improved and the leaden messengers whistled uncomfortably close, the warrior would be seen to cast himself over on the opposite side of the pony until his foot on the back and his face under the neck of the pony were all that could be seen, the rest of his person being completely covered by the body of the pony. This maneuver would frequently deceive the recruits among the soldiers; having fired probably about the time the warrior was seen to disappear, the recruit would shout exultingly and call attention of his comrades to his lucky shot. The old soldiers, however, were not so easily deceived, and often afterwards would remind their less experienced companion of the terrible fatality of his shots.

After finding that their plan to induce a small party to pursue them did not succeed, the Indians withdrew their forces and, concealment being no longer necessary, we were enabled to see their full numbers as that portion of them which had hitherto remained hidden behind a bluff rode boldly out on the open plain. Beyond rifle range, they contented themselves with taunts and with gestures of defiance then rode away.

From the officers of the camp I learned that the performance of the Indians which had occupied our attention on this afternoon was of almost daily occurrence and that the savages, from having been allowed to continue in their course unmolested, had almost reduced the camp to a state of siege; so true had this become that at no hour of the day was it safe for individuals to pass beyond the immediate limits of the camp.

Straightway Custer prepared to strike back. He led a sortie all the way to the old council ground on Medicine Lodge Creek, but the only Indians he could find, after days of searching, were those who slashed at his flank and rear with impunity in the vicinity of his own camp. He was forced to turn back without striking a single blow. One more score to settle when he should be able to connect!

What a dismal beginning for the splendid record he had expected to make for himself when he hurried from the East in answer to Sheridan's telegram! Sully's failure had been attributed to faulty, hesitant leadership. Custer had been expected to remedy the situation. Yet Sully had found Indians and had followed them deep into their southern retreat. Custer had searched in vain, had stopped short of the point reached by his predecessor and had been made to look more or less ridiculous in the eyes of those who had expected so much of him.

It was galling to his pride, a spur to preparations for the major offensive then being organized. It was a goad to the vicious element in his makeup. In the future, though he might not be able to catch and punish warriors in open warfare, such as the red knights insisted on making, he certainly could account for many women and children. His subsequent actions and his still later writings, as well as testimony of some of those who followed him, show that in the campaign now near at hand all Indians were to be treated alike. There was to be little distinction between warriors and noncombatants or age or sex.

For two weeks Custer and his force camped on

the banks of the Arkansas awaiting winter and orders to move into the enemy's country. Custer reorganized and drilled his cavalrymen. He acquired a group of Osages as guides during this period. Then came orders to prepare to move in and establish a base for operations before the weather should become too severe. It was to be a rather pretentious base, with supplies sufficient to subsist more than two thousand men six months, if necessary. Four hundred wagons were to accompany the expedition for the purpose of transporting this immense store of food and equipment.

A spot near the confluence of Beaver Creek and Wolf Creek had been tentatively agreed upon. It had been recommended by John Smith, veteran scout, who had piloted the Sully thrust past that location in September. It was approximately one hundred miles due south of Fort Dodge, well within the enemy's country, yet close enough to Fort Dodge to enable further transportation of necessary supplies. There was ideal terrain for a large camp, water aplenty and timber from which logs could be obtained for construction of the proposed stockade.

The long journey was made by this immense train without untoward incident. Once an Indian trail was struck. Absence of travois marks indicated it was that of a war party. Scouts estimated the number of this war party might be as great as one hundred. The trail came from the southwest and headed in a northeasterly direction.

Reasoning that this band probably was composed of most of the effectives of some village, Custer begged Sully to permit him to take the back trail and attack the village while its defenders were absent. This request, however, Sully refused.

Those who steadfastly have accused Custer of showing little distinction between warriors and women and children during his Washita campaign point to this incident as partial proof, at least, that he was determined from the beginning to treat all Indians alike. They also call attention to the fact that Custer did not, at least at that time, believe the war party had designs against the white settlements, as alleged in his memoirs, for a few days later he wrote Mrs. Custer:

> The day that we reached here (Camp Supply) we crossed a fresh trail of a large war party going north. Had the Kansas Volunteers been here, as we expected, my orders would have allowed me to follow the back trail of the war party right to their village and we would have found the latter in an unprotected state as their warriors had evidently gone north, either to (Fort) Larned or (Fort) Zarah, or to fight the Osage or Kaw Indians, who are now putting up their winter meat.

Shortly after arrival of this column at the spot selected for a base of operations, General Sheridan and his staff joined it. Sheridan brought news that the regiment of volunteers from Kansas was on its way. It was expected to augment the expedition within a few days. Taking supreme command, Sheridan sent Sully back to Kansas, instructing him to report for duty at Fort Harker.

The Kansas regiment, of which Sheridan spoke, was the Nineteenth Kansas Volunteer Cavalry. It has been authorized by the War Department to serve six months against the Indians south of the Arkansas. Not long did it take Governor Samuel J. Crawford to recruit the twelve companies authorized. Authorization was received the second week in October. By the first week in November, all units had been completed, equipped and were ready to be mustered in at Topeka. Governor Crawford, in person, was to lead this regiment. He resigned as the state's chief executive to do so. As time for its departure arrived, two companies were ordered to Fort Hays to serve as an escort for General Sheridan and staff.

The other ten were to march overland for the field base at the junction of Beaver and Wolf creeks.

From Topeka to Camp Supply, as the new base had been named, was a much longer jaunt than those in charge had supposed. The route lay past the mouth of the Little Arkansas, where Wichita now stands, to Medicine Lodge Creek and thence to the ultimate destination. Five days, it was estimated, would be sufficient to make the journey. Consequently only rations for that period were sent along. Five days subsistence for horses and mules was deemed ample. All these supplies became exhausted long before the troops reached the Cimarron.

At first there was no great concern. Grasses furnished subsistence for animals. The men fared handsomely upon buffalo meat obtained from bands of these shaggy beasts encountered on the way. Four days out from Medicine Lodge Creek a severe snowstorm swept down from the North. At that time the cavalcade had just sighted the bluffs of the Cimarron. It was known that their objective was a considerable distance beyond that stream.

Now deeply concerned over the situation, Colonel Crawford sent a picked scouting party to see if it could find their destination. If successful, it was to urge Sheridan to rush forage for the horses and supplies for the men. The Colonel realized horses would be hard put to find anything to eat if, as now seemed very likely, the snowstorm should continue long.

Not only did the snowstorms continue, but it increased in intensity during the night. The entire command remained in camp next day for fear of losing its way in the blinding blizzard. Finally the march was resumed. By now the snow was more than a foot deep. So weak had become the horses from exposure and from lack of food that the men had to walk and lead them. Save for hackberries, which they found in great abundance, the men, too, would have gone without anything to eat after reaching the breaks of the Cimarron.

By this time, too, teams of the wagon train had become completely exhausted. Some of the men became ill. It was impossible for the entire command to continue. Selecting those best fitted for the task, Colonel Crawford placed half his men in charge of Captain David L. Payne[7] and consented to their pushing on. The Colonel remained behind with the remainder of his men.

Three days later Captain Payne led his staggering troopers into Camp Supply. There he learned the original scouting party sent ahead had reached its goal and supplies had been sent back to those left stranded on the banks of the Cimarron.

Eventually the last of the Kansans arrived at their destination. There they began making preparations for the next move.

But that next move awaited the return of Custer and the Seventh Cavalry which already had departed on its first scout of this campaign.

7. Captain David L. Payne, commander of Company H., Nineteenth Kansas Volunteer Cavalry on this occasion, later was to become famous by attempting to colonize portions of the Indian country before Congress had opened this region to White settlement.

CHAPTER SIX
Along the Washita

TAPPING the plains of Texas only a few miles south of the main Canadian River, rises what once was a beautiful, clear water stream. Paralleling its broad-channeled neighbor almost to the ninety-seventh meridian, it suddenly swings south past the Arbuckle Mountains, then east and south again, forming the borderline between Marshall and Bryan counties before emptying into Red River.

Unlike most of the Plains rivers, its narrow channel runs deep, confined between rather precipitous banks. It drains one of the most fertile valleys in all of Oklahoma.

From its source to its mouth it is fringed with heavy growths of a variety of trees, preponderantly cottonwoods, elms and hackberries. All of its main tributaries also are wooded.

Along its banks grow an equally large variety of bushes, tall grasses, luxuriant short grasses, shrubs and wild flowers.

As far back as tradition runs and history records, it was a wildlife paradise. In this region vast herds of buffalo were accustomed to winter. Here was forage, not only along the main stream, but also along its numerous tributaries. Here was protection from sweeping winds. Deer, antelope, wild turkey, pinnated grouse and quail abounded. Game animals and game birds in countless thousands never left its environs.

Because of this remarkable abundance of game, the stream derived its name from Choctaw words meaning "Big Hunt." Choctaws and Chickasaws and others of the Five Civilized Tribes had hunted its southern and eastern extremities more than a century ago. Small parties sometimes risked conflicts with the Plains tribes by venturing far up its course. From the easternmost slope of the Wichitas to the plains of Texas it was the favorite hunting ground of the Kiowas and Comanches and Lipans, or Plains Apaches. These tribesmen ranged south, west and north. It furnished part of the fare for remnants of the Caddo and Wichita tribes. From the North came bands of Cheyennes and Arapahoes in ever-increasing numbers to lay in a winter's supply of meat, especially after overland trails of commerce and projecting railroads had begun to drive buffalo from the regions of the Missouri, the Platte and the Arkansas.

As the vanguard of white man's civilization pushed westward through Fort Smith and Fort Gibson, military posts followed. Not far from the mouth of the Washita was established a post known as Fort Washita. Farther north, at the eastern edge of the Arbuckle uplift near where the Washita pushes its way through a break in this elevation, was located Fort Arbuckle, the farthest outpost of any consequence at the close of the Civil War. True, a makeshift military camp once had been established halfway between the ninety-eighth and ninety-ninth meridians on Pond Creek about a mile above where this tributary enters the Washita. It had consisted of only a few adobe structures and had been abandoned at the outbreak of the conflict between the North and the South. It was known as Fort Cobb.

Treaties of the Little Arkansas and Medicine Lodge drew civilization's lines closer to this region from the North. In their crude way of recognizing boundaries, the Cheyennes, Arapahoes, Kiowas and Comanches considered all of the area between the

COMANCHE VILLAGE ON THE WASHITA

Red River on the south and the Arkansas on the north as their legitimate range. Hunting was fair along the North Fork of the Canadian, the Cimarron, the Arkansas and the main Canadian during the summer months but, with one accord, these tribes assembled in winter along the upper reaches of the Washita. This was far from the soldiers at Fort Arbuckle to the south and east. It was far from interference by Texans pushing up toward the panhandle of their state. It was remote from the soldiers at Fort Dodge, recently established on the Arkansas to the north.

Here the valley of the Washita was flanked by red-studded hills. The stream wound its way through the valley here in a series of great bends, offering dense tree protection against the elements on three sides.

It was in the area just south and east of the Antelope Hills, in what is now Roger Mills County, that practically all of the tribes signatory to the Medicine Lodge peace past were congregated for the winter of 1868-69.

Under the terms of this treaty the Government was to issue annuities to these five tribes. Fort Cobb suggested itself as the most logical location for the agency. General Hazen had been designated to take charge of this service. Entering the region through Fort Smith and Fort Gibson, he had proceeded to Fort Arbuckle where he was furnished a squadron of cavalry and a company of infantry as an escort and garrison for his post. He had installed the agency early in November following signing of the treaty.

That autumn the tribes had been camped in a series of deep bends immediately south of the Antelope Hills. Later they had moved down stream several miles to the vicinity of the present site of the city of Cheyenne, county seat of Roger Mills County.

Black Kettle had selected a site farther west than any of the others. His was an ideal location. A high ridge rose to the south, a higher one to the north, their summits being scarcely two miles apart. His chosen campsite was flanked on the west by a tree-fringed branch of the Washita. Below him another tributary flowed through a break in the southern hills. At the western edge of the flat bottom, the Washita made a small sweep to the north, came back south and then formed a larger horseshoe bend to the north. South of these two comparatively small bends an elevation rose rather precipitously. The westernmost protected pocket was ideal for Black Kettle's winter camping purposes. It was just large enough to accommodate the three-score lodges of his immediate following. Ample forage for the herds of the village was to be found in the ravines to the west.

Black Kettle had chosen for his lodge site a spot under a giant cottonwood tree on the river bank at the western extremity of the smaller of the two bends. Only one was farther west than his. It was that of Big Man, a blood relative of Black Kettle and father of the budding warrior, Magpie. A few others had pitched their tepees in that vicinity, but the greater part of the village was located in the larger bend, a snug, cozy camp.

As winter came on, the pony herds were collected from their wider range on every side to browse and graze in the ravines, sandhills and groves upstream. Their trail from the main village crossed the Washita near Black Kettle's lodge, where an easy fording of the stream was possible. From here it ran west through the immediate sandhills to the main foraging area.

Conformation of the river and crowding hills prevented other villages being established in the immediate vicinity; but two miles farther down stream the Washita swept to the north and east in a tremendous oxbow loop more than a mile deep. Inside this loop the land was almost as level as a floor. Along the western side, that nearest Black Kettle's band, Little Raven's Arapahoes installed themselves. Earlier in the autumn, Kiowas under Satanta, Lone Wolf and Black Eagle also had been camped there, but recently had moved to the vicinity of Fort Cobb, leaving behind some thirty lodges of Kicking Bird's band, the only Kiowas on the upper reaches of the Washita. These occupied part of the huge bend with the Arapahoes. In a succession of smaller bends just below, Medicine Arrow's Cheyennes, Little Robe's Cheyennes, more Arapahoes, a few Apaches and Comanches populated the valley a distance of several miles. In all, more than six thousand tribesmen were encamped there at the beginning of the winter of 1868. Along the Washita, between Black Kettle's village and Fort Cobb, were nearly all of the other non-reservation Indians of the Southern Plains.

Their fall hunt had been eminently successful. Curing strips of buffalo meat hung from every lodgepole. Piles of cured buffalo hides waited final dressing and crude manufacture into garments, robes or lodge coverings. Huntsmen and warriors whiled away the time shaping new bows, shafting arrows, running bullets and puffing on their long-stemmed pipes.

Periodical trips to Fort Cobb to visit the new agency, obtain supplies and confer with the representative of the Great White Father broke the monotony of camp life.

The Indians liked Hazen. His friendly attitude, his sympathetic understanding of their problems drew them to him. Already some of the older chiefs were beginning to be interested in the plans he told them the Great White Father in Washington was making for their future security. The white man's road might not be so hard to travel, after all, they concluded. Relations between Indians and Whites would not have been so strained if the other soldier chiefs understood the red men as well as did most of the agents the Great White Father had sent out to deal with them such as Hazen, Leavenworth, Wynkoop.

Soon after the beginning of their acquaintance with this new agent, the southern tribesmen learned disquieting news from him. Some of the Whites were using summer raids by detached hostile bands as an excuse for attempting to force all Indians to accept and remain on more restricted reservations. There they would be compelled to till the soil, to build houses, to learn other trades, to learn to read and write and to live like white men, forsaking the chase as a major livelihood. Three columns of troops at that very hour were moving against them from as many directions, they were told.

The Indians protested. They explained that there still was plenty of game south of the Arkansas in the region given them as inviolate hunting grounds under terms of the peace pact signed on Medicine Lodge Creek. They wanted to continue to live as their forefathers had lived, as they had been promised they could live.

Would not Hazen, who knew what the head men of the tribes told him was so, inform the white war chiefs they were friendly? Would he not command the soldiers not to molest them in their distant retreat?

Sadly, Hazen shook his head. To the pleading chieftains he replied that he did not have the authority to command the white war chiefs then in the field to turn back. He could, however, advise them the Indians along the Washita were striving to live up to their agreements made during the big talk on Medicine Lodge Creek.

Late in November a party from Black Kettle's village talked with Hazen about these things. This party included Black Kettle, Big Man, father of Magpie, Wolf Looking Back, father of Little Beaver, and Little Rock, he whose lodge on the east side of Black Kettle's camp was so highly decorated by many painted figures and by trophies of warpath and chase. They received little consolation.[1]

The heavens to the north were leaden as if reflecting the gloom of these warriors' spirits as the little group of Cheyennes set forth on the long return trek to their camp. Each carried with him sugar, coffee, tobacco and hard crackers given them by their agent. Snow flurries which struck Fort Cobb during their visit increased to blizzard proportions as they pushed into the teeth of the north wind. Progress was slow. It was not until nightfall of November 26 that they reached their destination.

That night Big Man and Magpie ate a belated

---

1. Quoting from General Hazen's report of June 30, 1869, as he prepared to close his duties at Camp Wichita, Report of Commissioner of Indian Affairs, 1869, page 390:

"Soon after arriving I received a copy of the instructions to Major General Sheridan, directing him to pursue and punish the Indians which had been depredating in Kansas, even into the reservations under my charge and to Fort Cobb should it become necessary. As he was then in the Indian country, not in communication with me, but in pursuit of the Indians that had been depredating in Kansas, and having made extensive preparations and being fully determined upon a successful campaign, with full authority to carry it even into my camp, it became imperative that I should bring there the Indians that had been a war in Kansas, proffering an apparent security while inviting an attack upon my own people and virtually driving to the Plains the Indians actually at peace, and setting back our real work for years. So when Black Kettle with a delegation of his people and the Arapahoes came to Fort Cobb to make peace, I told them I had not the power to make peace . . I advised all who really wanted peace to return without delay to their camps, to call their people in from the warpath and to avoid the threatening war by watchfulness. . . . They returned to their camps then on the Washita about eighty miles above Fort Cobb."

supper with Black Kettle in the head chief's lodge. They drank coffee with sugar in it and munched hard crackers along with their repast of buffalo meat. The talk was all about the disquieting news they had learned from Hazen—that soldiers were making a winter campaign to punish all the tribes for some depredations a few reckless young men had committed that autumn when they had slipped away from their villages for an unauthorized warpath.

Before they had finished their meal, it had been decided that Black Kettle would summon his leading men for a council that night. He would advise them of the bad news he had heard and would counsel with them about sending a delegation to have a talk with the soldier chiefs as soon as the snow, which then covered the ground a depth of more than a foot, should go away. Though the soldiers might be headed in that direction, surely they would not attempt to move with such a blizzard raging.

The council was called.[2] Far into the night it lasted. The head men of the village decided to move down among the neighboring villages for better mutual protection as soon as possible. At the same time, runners would be sent to the soldiers coming from the north, requesting a talk about the situation. There must be some misunderstanding that could be adjusted satisfactorily, they reasoned.

Meanwhile, in another tepee, a small and unofficial council was being held. Crow Neck was telling Bad Man, in whose lodge he was living, what he had seen several miles up the Washita that day. Crow Neck was one of those who had slipped away to join

2. Custer says in his "Life on the Plains," page 227, that the village was awake until after midnight celebrating a successful raid made by a party from that camp which had just returned. The activity in camp that night undoubtedly was the result of the disturbing information Black Kettle and his associates had brought back from Fort Cobb.

the party whose trail Elliott had discovered and had
followed.

Crow Neck was saying that, when the returning
party had struck the Washita several miles upstream the previous day, the horse he was riding became exhausted from the long, hard ride in deep
snow. So Crow Neck had led him into the timber
and had tied him to a bush, intending to go back and
get him the next day. When Crow Neck had gone
back for his horse, as he was nearing the spot where
he had left it, he looked to the north and saw what
he thought were soldiers in the far distance. Afraid
to continue on to the place where he had left his
horse, Crow Neck had turned back. He had come
straight to Bad Man to counsel with him as to
whether he should tell the village what he had seen.

His host was inclined to doubt the objects Crow
Neck had seen were soldiers. Likely they were buffalo. Crow Neck's conscience, Bad Man suggested,
might be bothering him, because he had slipped
away from the tribe for a warpath when he knew
the chiefs did not want him to go, and that he had
been "seeing things." Later, however, Bad Man
became more concerned. He sent his squaws after
his horses, preparatory to moving his belongings to
one of the lower camps on the morrow.

Crow Neck did not spread the alarm any farther.
He was afraid some might laugh at him. Then there
was the further fear that he might get into trouble
if Black Kettle should learn that he had been with a
raiding party.

But for this timidity on the part of Crow Neck,
the village might have been saved and Custer's
Washita campaign might have had an entirely different ending. History might have been changed.

Still another group in camp sensed that all was
not right. This was a family of Sioux. Overtaken
by the snowstorm, while visiting friends along the

Washita, the Sioux had pitched their tepee with those of Black Kettle's village. When the Sioux learned from those returning from Fort Cobb of the possible coming of the soldiers, he suggested no time be lost in moving to a place of greater safety. Especially concerned were the other members of his family, his wife and three daughters. They finally decided to move their lodge back to one of the lower villages next day.

CHAPTER SEVEN

On to The Washita

$\mathcal{P}$ATIENCE never was a Custer virtue. Delay fretted this impetuous young general, always eager for action. As days passed with no word from the long-overdue Kansans, he importuned General Sheridan to permit him to set forth in search of those they had come to chastise.

Finally, Sheridan yielded. He promised Custer that if the missing regiment did not put in appearance before night he could take all available troops and head south. Sheridan, himself would await the coming of the volunteers. As soon as the Kansans had recuperated from the arduous march they then were completing, they would follow Custer. They were to take a more easterly course, eventually connecting with the Seventh in the vicinity of Fort Cobb if no hostiles were encountered in the meantime.

Throughout that day the Seventh made ready for a thirty-day scout. Each trooper saw that all his equipment was in shape and that his horse was well shod. Wagons were loaded with supplies.

By mid-day the thermometer was sinking steadily. Leaden skies, drifting down from the North, began to spit snow. The same blizzard which had stalled the Kansas regiment struck Camp Supply with full force that night. Sheridan and Custer had wanted a winter campaign. The weather had obliged them.

It was a grumbling, profanely protesting command that was awakened long before daylight the morning of November 23, 1868, by the unwelcome notes of reveille. No one was more profane than

Custer as he sought to hasten departure. It was a shivering, swearing bunch of muleskinners which hooked up the transport wagons in snow nearly knee deep. Snow was still descending. The north wind penetrated even the heaviest clothing.

Among the early risers was Custer. Sheridan stuck to his bunk with its blankets and buffalo robes. There Custer found him as he called to say good-bye and receive final instructions.[1]

"Kill or hang every warrior. Bring back all women and children. Take good care of yourself," were the senior commander's parting orders.

The entourage which departed camp at daybreak consisted of eleven companies of the Seventh Cavalry numbering some eight hundred effectives, a detachment of white, half-breed and Indian scouts, and a creaking, groaning wagon train.

Every man had dressed for warmth, little heed being paid to appearances. Custer, himself, was engulfed in a huge overcoat. His feet were encased in overshoes made of buffalo hide with the hair inside. His hands were muffled in fur-lined mittens.

Originally, Custer had planned to head north, there picking up and backtracking the Indian trail observed a few days previously. Now snow obliterated that trail. Acting on the advice of Ben Clark, his new chief of scouts, a course was laid up Wolf Creek in a southwesterly direction. Custer pro-

1. D. B. Randolph Keim's "Sheridan Troopers," page 103, relates:
"The instructions issued for the expedition were brief and simple: 'To proceed South in the direction of the Antelope Hills, thence toward the Washita river, the supposed Winter seat of the hostile tribes; to destroy their villages and ponies, to kill or hang all warriors, and bring back all women and children."
"Grandma" Mason, a daughter of one of the Camp Supply teamsters told the writer in 1930 that she often heard those who accompanied Custer on the Washita expedition say their orders were to "kill every topknot."

posed to continue in that direction until directly
north of the Antelope Hills, best known landmark in
that region. Then, if no signs of Indians had been
discovered in the meantime, the column would swing
south and east toward Fort Cobb.

So difficult was progress, as a result of the deep
snow, that only fifteen miles were covered the first
day. The command went into camp in heavy timber along the banks of Wolf Creek. For three days
Custer clung to this valley. No Indian village, no
trail having been discovered, the cavalcade turned
south and headed for the Canadian in the vicinity of
the Antelope Hills.

Beyond lay the valley of the Washita. Here, in
the opinion of Ben Clark, California Joe and other
scouts, most likely would be found the winter camps
of the hostiles, for this region was considered far
more suitable for winter needs of the Indians than
that of the bleak Canadian.

The Canadian was reached. Its broad channel,
partly frozen over, presented a difficult problem for
the expedition, particularly the wagon train. Realizing several hours would be required to make the
crossing, Custer determined to send a scouting party westward in search of possible Indian signs.

To Major Elliott fell this assignment. Accompanied by a small detachment, this trusted officer
set forth. Twelve miles upstream, almost to the
Texas border, Elliott discovered a comparatively
fresh trail. It headed slightly east of south. It was
believed to mark the return of the same party
whose trail had been seen while Sully was moving his
train and troopers from Fort Dodge to establish
Camp Supply. The pony tracks indicated the party
was moving two abreast. There was no sign of travois
trails which would have been found had a village
on the move passed that way.

Immediately, Elliott dispatched Jack Corbin, one

of his best mounted scouts, to inform Custer of the discovery. By the same messenger Custer sent word back to Elliott to stick to the trail, advising him, further, that the remainder of the troops would take a short cut and join him as soon as possible. Leaving a suitable guard to escort the wagon train, Custer speeded up his column. Elliott had passed when Custer finally ran into the trail, rapid as his march had been. It was long after nightfall before the advance scouting party was overtaken. It was discovered encamped in a heavily wooded cove on the banks of the Washita awaiting the main command.

Certainly the village could not be far distant. Believing he could find it before long, and the night being light, Custer decided to push forward as soon as a brief halt had been made to rest and feed horses and men. This accomplished with the least possible delay, advance was resumed. Scouts moved afoot far ahead of the column. Every other precaution was taken to proceed as quietly and as swiftly as possible.

Two hours passed. Then the Osages ahead reported discovery of a small fire in one of the many ravines leading from the ridge at the left into the Washita at the right. It apparently had been abandoned only a short time previously. Brief examination of the grove revealed prints of many pony hoofs in the trampled snow. From the signs, scouts concluded the fire had been built there by the Indian boys tending a large herd of ponies as the animals browsed around for what scant forage could be obtained. Evidently it had been abandoned when night came on and the boys had driven their charges back close to the village until morning. All knew now that their journey's end was near.

Caution was redoubled. Head scouts never crossed a ridge without first creeping to the summit to peer

CAMP SUPPLY

A. Billinghau

cautiously over. The village might be just beyond
any of them.

At last they made the long-anticipated discovery.
In the distance a dog barked. A tinkling bell revealed proximity of the pony herd. Strain their eyes
as they might, however, the scouts could not see any
lodges in the then brilliant starlight. But they knew
that not far away, screened by the heavy growth of
timber in the valley below them, stood the village
they sought.

Custer was signaled to join them. Passing back
word for the column to halt, he did so. His pulse
quickened as his ears, rather than his eyes, told him
his goal had been reached. Had not the barking of
the dogs and the tinkling of the pony bell been sufficient, all doubt was dispelled when the cry of an Indian child floated up from below. Later, in com-
menting on the thoughts which raced through his
head as he continued his observations, Custer wrote:

> I could not but regret that in a war, such as we
> were forced to engage in, the mode and circumstances
> of battle would possibly prevent discrimination (be-
> tween warriors, women and children.)

Presently the reconnoitering group was joined
by Ben Clark. Still none was able to determine
whether the village was on the south side of the
stream or between the soldiers and the Washita, or
possibly, on both sides of the river, snugly protected
by the timber.

Ben Clark was assigned the precarious task of
establishing its definite location. Taking with him
Jack Corbin and Romero, he set out on this hazardous mission. Silently, stealthily, they made their way
into the valley. Moving cautiously so as not to disturb the pony herd nor to alarm the ever-alert curs
of the camp, they progressed to the river's bank.
From there the entire village was plainly visible. It
was spread out over a broad flat just beyond the
trees for a distance of perhaps a quarter of a mile.

Beyond rose a precipitous embankment, and beyond that lay a narrow plateau. All tepees were on the southern side of the river. Against the horizon to the south was sharply defined a ridge similar to that which concealed Custer's command on the north. Here and there pointed knolls punctured the skyline. Romero was sent into the camp itself for a more complete investigation.

The scouts retraced their steps to Custer, undetected. To him they made known their discoveries. They estimated the fighting strength of the village to be scarcely one-fifth that of the soldiers.

Custer was not long determining his plan of attack. This time there would be no opportunity for his intended victims to escape by flight. Before morning he could surround the village. At a given signal the encircling battle line would converge on the unsuspecting Indians, who then would be completely at his mercy. It would be a wipe-out.

Word was sent to his command to make itself as comfortable as possible without fires. To light fires might prove fatal to hopes of a surprise attack. Subordinate officers, troop commanders were ordered to join the general at his observation post that they might reconnoiter the situation while receiving instructions for the contemplated charge.

The terrain admirably suited Custer's purposes. To the left, the ridge, behind which they were hidden from the village, rose to even greater heights directly opposite the camp. This offered a perfect screen for an encircling move in that direction. To the right, it sloped down into the wooded valley of the Washita. A dark line extending into the horizon, in that direction, gave evidence of a ravine up which troops could move to the rear of the village, yet keep out of sight of any who might be astir among the lodges.

To Major Elliott fell the lot of leading three companies ordered to make the circling march around the village from the left. This detachment set out immediately, for theirs was the longest journey. Further, some time might be required to find a suitable break in the ridge through which his forces could descend into the valley. Little more than a mile had been covered when Elliott, taking Captain Barnitz with him, advanced to the summit of the ridge to view the territory below. There, concealed behind a rugged peak, they made their survey of the situation. Not far ahead loomed a break in the ridge behind which they had been advancing eastward. This ravine would throw them into the valley just far enough below the sleeping village to avoid detection, yet close enough to strike quickly when time came to launch the assault. They returned to their troopers and moved out, entering the valley through the break they had discovered.

Within an hour, Elliott had deployed his command. Some were dismounted as soon as they reached the timber. These were instructed to move forward among the trees, afoot. The remainder continued on south after crossing the stream to take up their position behind a low rise on that side. They were directly opposite the point where Custer's main command would ride in.

Colonel Thompson drew an assignment to encircle the village from the west, with two companies, crossing the Washita and moving up the lateral ravine which had been sighted from Custer's first observation point. All of his men retained their mounts, for they had open territory across which they must charge when the battle should commence. Their right wing was to contact Elliott's left.

Closing the gap between Colonel Thompson's detachment and the main force were two companies in charge of Colonel Myers. Part of Myers' men were to advance through the timber along the banks of the Washita to cut off escape in that direction.

The remainder, four companies of cavalry, all of the Osage and white scouts and forty sharpshooters under Colonel Cook, were retained as Custer's personal command. This was much the strongest force. Cook's sharpshooters were to dismount upon reaching the timber and deploy through the trees. This mode of fighting was calculated to be more effective than shooting from horseback.

Each detachment was under orders to charge at daybreak.

CHAPTER EIGHT

The Washita Massacre

*O*RDINARILY, Plains Indians were in no hurry to crawl from between warm buffalo robes on cold winter mornings. They had few early chores demanding such inconvenience. It was bitterly cold the morning of November 27, 1868; but those who had come from Fort Cobb the previous day brought news of such a disturbing nature as to set many astir in the village of Black Kettle at daylight. Despite lateness of his retirement the previous night, Black Kettle, himself, was one of the early risers. He was filled with forebodings.

Emerging from the low entrance to his lodge and straightening to his full height of slightly less than six feet, he let his eyes rove about the village. Beyond tops of the tepeês in the bend east of him the sky was brightening, heralding the rising of the sun. Wisps of smoke curled from apertures at the apex of more than one lodge. To the north the rugged snow-covered knolls of the flanking ridge loomed dimly through the barren branches of the intervening trees and a heavy blanket of fog. To the south it was one solid landscape of white, rising less sharply than that on the other side of the Washita. The scene was peaceful enough.

Suddenly an Indian woman burst into view, running down the pony trail on the opposite side of the stream as fast as frightened moccasin feet could carry her.

"Soldiers! Soldiers" she cried as she saw the figure of Black Kettle outside his lodge.

Back into his lodge plunged the chief. Immediately he reappeared, rifle in hand. By that time the breathless messenger had splashed through the ford and was standing in front of him gasping her story.

The master of her lodge having decided the night before to move down to one of the other villages as soon as possible, she had gone to fetch the family horses. While moving up the trail through the timber, she had heard horses approaching. At first she thought it might be the pony herd coming down to camp. An instant later she caught a glimpse of soldiers moving rapidly toward her. Without stopping long enough to estimate the size of the party or to attempt to identify it, beyond assuring herself it was a body of mounted soldiers, she had sped back to camp to give the alarm.

Was the mission of the soldiers one of peace or war? This unheralded visit in the dead of winter, its surreptitious approach, recalled vividly to Black Kettle's mind another late November morning four years previously when, also at the earliest break of day, Chivington had led a murdering horde into Black Kettle's camp on Sand Creek under very similar circumstances.

Painful recollections of his own narrow escape, the death and mutilation of so many of his tribesmen on that occasion, caused the head chief to resolve that his village this time would not wait to be fired upon before taking flight. He would arouse the camp and then delay the soldiers as long as possible by a parley at the ford, for he stood directly in the path of their approach. Ordering the woman to go through the village and cry the alarm, Black Kettle pointed his gun in air and pulled the trigger to awaken those who might still be asleep.[1]

Meanwhile, hearing the excited voice of the woman and Black Kettle's sharp commands, those in nearby lodges had scrambled from their abodes, sensing something was wrong. Told of approaching soldiers, they, too, sped away to aid in arousing the village.

Big Man had just stepped out of his lodge and Magpie was sticking an antiquated pistol and a knife into his belt when he heard the report of Black Kettle's rifle. Magpie hurried out.

It was customary for important men of the tribe to keep a pony or two tethered near their lodges for emergency use or convenience, so that it would not be necessary to go to the main herd every time a mount was desired. One was staked near Black Kettle's tepee. As Magpie slipped from his father's lodge, he saw Black Kettle's wife untie this pony and lead it up to her master. At that instant came a trumpet's blast from the timber in the direction of the advancing soldiers. Shouted commands, an ear-splitting cheer, a thunder of hoofs and a crashing of underbrush left no doubt of the hostile nature of this visit. Answering shouts from all sides of the village also told the chief that his camp was being charged from every side. His rifle was empty. He had not reloaded after firing his warning shot. He could not offer armed resistance.

Leaping to the back of his pony and pulling his faithful squaw up behind him, Black Kettle made a dash for the ford, hoping to beat the soldiers to it and make his escape down the north side of the channel.

Even as he dug heels into his pony's sides and gave it the word, the head of the charging column, led by Custer, himself, burst into view a few yards ahead. Came a volley from pistols and carbines. Black Kettle felt a burning sting in the pit of his stomach. One bullet had found its mark. He swerved to the right, still riding for the stream. Another slug struck him in the back between his shoulder blades just as his pony splashed into the channel. He collapsed, sliding into the water, dead. On dashed his thoroughly frightened horse. By the time it reached the top of the opposite bank, it was riderless. Black Kettle's wife had entered the happy hunting grounds on the heels of her illustrious mate.

Thus, the greatest of all Cheyenne chieftains, first in war in the days when he thought the Indians might successfully resist seizure of their lands, and first in peace when he became convinced of the futility of this unequal struggle, became the first to fall in Custer's raid on the Washita.

On into the startled village raced Custer's men, shouting, shooting, slashing. Pistols were discharged in the very faces of incredulous Indians as they thrust heads from their lodges to ascertain the cause of all this commotion. Sabres struck down others. Any head which appeared was an immediate target, whether that of warrior, woman or child. A warrior leveled his pistol at Custer. Custer beat him to the shot. The Indian fell, pierced through the head. Ben Clark, who stuck to the side of his chief until Custer quit personal participation in the fighting, said that was the only Indian slain by Custer, personally, during the entire engagement.

Those on the far side of the village, attempting to escape in that direction, ran into the charging troopers of Elliott, Thompson, or Myers, which had completed their encircling movement before Custer opened the attack. No quarter was shown in that first wild dash by the converging lines of horsemen. After that opening assault there was little semblance of military formations. It was for every man to make the most of his individual opportunities.

Especially active were the Osages. Not in years had they enjoyed such a glorious opportunity to vent their blood-lust on their hereditary enemies. Scalping knives soon were dripping. Nor were their wielders satisfied with the mere lifting of scalps. Breasts of their women victims were slashed. Arms and

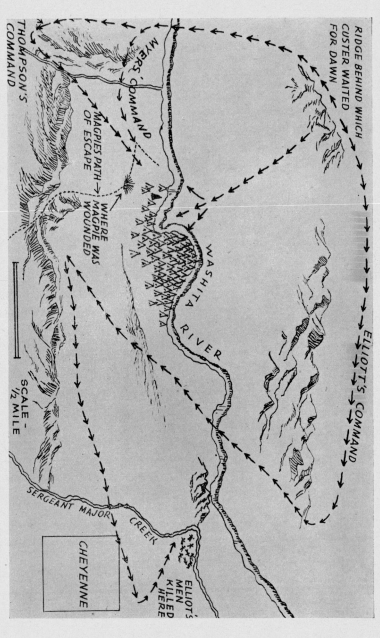

MAP SHOWING MOVEMENTS OF CUSTER'S TROOPS IN BATTLE OF THE WASHITA

legs were severed and bodies otherwise mutilated.

Some of Custer's troopers could not resist the temptation to belt their first Indian scalps.

Soon soldiers began to group in pursuit of fleeing foemen. From every side came the heavy report of carbines. Occasionally an Indian rifle answered. But these were notable for their infrequency. So sudden had been the attack, only a few of the red men had opportunity to arm themselves. Most of those who did so had only bows and arrows. They were powerless to offer serious resistance. Flight was their only objective.

Those villagers whose tepees stood nearest the stream fared better than their friends in the center and on the south side of the camp. First to dash through the icy waters of the Washita and scramble up the opposite bank found themselves running into scouts and sharpshooters who had deployed in the timber there. They also encountered troopers, mounted and dismounted. Seeing escape shut off in that direction, the fugitives accepted the only avenue left open to them, the channel itself. It was misery to wade its ice-fringed waters, but it was either that or bullets.

Women and children, as well as braves, plunged into the stream. Most of them were scantily clad. Many were without moccasins on their feet. Frequently the water reached to the armpits of adults who had to carry the children through these deep pools to prevent their drowning. Desperately they splashed their way beyond the lines of their enemies. Eventually they made their way, half dead from exposure, exhaustion and fright, to the Arapahoe village of Little Raven below. Here they found refuge. Here they were given dry clothing and food and found relief before the blazing fires of friendly neighbors.

While Custer's own version of this attack would

lead one to believe his troops received spirited resistance from heavily armed Indians, who promptly rushed to cover of the timber and opened fire on the soldiers from ambush, the fact that only Captain Hamilton was killed and only eleven soldiers were wounded during the sacking of the village subject this portion of his narrative to serious doubt of its accuracy. Nor was it an Indian bullet which killed Hamilton.[1]

Perhaps the most "desperate resistance" encountered during the entire struggle for possession of the camp, if struggle it rightfully can be termed, was that offered by three Indians covering the flight of those fleeing in the stream. These three, protected by the trunk of a fallen tree, drove back the soldiers who attempted to follow those in the water. In spite of the fact that only one was armed with a rifle, the other two possessing only bows and arrows, they succeeded in checking pursuit.

Most accounts agree that in less than an hour from commencement of the attack the village and

1. Captain Hamilton's coat, worn on that occasion, is to be found in the museum of the Oklahoma Historical Society, Oklahoma City. It was sent to the society by Captain Hamilton's brother, along with the cap and belt this young officer was wearing at the time he was killed. The coat shows a single bullet-hole in the back, bloodstained on the inside. There is no bullet-hole in the front.

Some of the white scouts, including Ben Clark, who was riding stirrup to stirrup with Custer on the opposite side to Hamilton when Hamilton fell, said some were inclined to believe it possible Hamilton was killed by a bullet intended for Custer by some of those immediately behind who "had it in for" the general because of his abusive disposition.

The most likely explanation of his death, however, is that Hamilton was struck by a poorly directed shot caused by the poor aim of troopers, the uneven nature of the ground over which they were galloping, and the excitement incident to commencement of firing.

Clark did not believe an Indian bullet was responsible, inasmuch as Hamilton was killed before the Indians had opened fire.

immediate vicinity had been cleared of warriors, that the only Indians remaining in contact with the soldiers were noncombatants who chose to hide in their lodges rather than risk their lives by flight. These are believed to have constituted the entire complement of prisoners, fifty-three in number, according to Custer's official report, he carried away with him when he retreated that night.

In addition to Black Kettle, only one other chief was killed during this engagement. This was Little Rock, second in rank, whose ornamented lodge stood at the lower end of the camp. Eleven other warriors who fell, according to the Indians, were without rank. If, as he reported, Custer counted one hundred and three Indian dead, the remainder were bound to have been women and children. Some believe the slaughter of noncombatants was even greater than Custer reported. One out of every five of the women and children he captured was wounded.

Personal experiences related by Magpie and Little Beaver were typical. No sooner was it apparent that the village was being attacked than Magpie, standing within a few feet of Black Kettle when Custer charged across the Washita, headed for the cover of a creek some three hundred yards south and west. Alongside him raced his father, Big Man, and another warrior, named Pushing Bear.

Halfway to their goal they saw Myer's men galloping from the very brush toward which they were heading. Turning south, they raced for a small clump of chinaberry bushes growing in a slight depression. Just as the fugitives reached its edge, troopers fired a volley after them, although they did not check their headlong dash for the village proper where the frantic inhabitants were running in every direction. One of these bullets struck Magpie in the calf of his leg, inflicting a painful but not disabling wound. That was the last Magpie saw of his father until after the battle.

Pushing Bear and Magpie, however, crept to the other side of their scant shelter. Noting that all troopers had centered their attention on the camp, they made a break for a low ridge farther south. If they could gain this objective, they could continue unobserved to the lower villages. They were nearing the protection of two pointed knolls when a single horseman spied them and gave chase. Limping from his wound and progressing slowly because of the deep, crusted snow, Magpie rapidly was being overhauled. His companion refused to leave him. Pushing Bear was unarmed. Magpie had only his cap-and-ball revolver and a knife. Yet they decided they would put up a fight when overtaken. Slipping his knife to Pushing Bear, Magpie pulled his ancient firearm from his belt as the soldier rode up. Dodging a sweeping sabre, Magpie suddenly thrust the muzzle of his pistol almost against the stomach of the soldier and pulled the trigger. The soldier slumped in his saddle. Magpie yanked him from his seat.[2]

Meantime, Pushing Bear had seized the horse's bridle. As the rider crashed into the snow, Pushing Bear assisted Magpie to mount. Then he swung to the horse's back behind Magpie. The horse was put to a run. Before the fugitives could gain the top of the ridge, however, a squad of troopers which came riding from the east gave chase. It was Major Elliott and his detachment which was destined soon to be surrounded and annihilated.

Seing that the fleeing pair would gain the crest ahead of them and likely would outstrip them, the soldiers turned their attention to a group of Indians escaping on foot between them and the river. To-

2. See Appendix I.

ward this group the soldiers rode. Halfway to this group they encountered a boy, named "Crazy," because of a mental affliction, and an old man. Both of these the soldiers killed.

Little Beaver, twelve years old at the time, came near forfeiting his life for the sake of a revolver his father, Wolf Looking Back, had given him. The lodge of Wolf Looking Back stood almost in the center of the village. It was so far removed from the point of first attack that all of his family could have made their escape had they so desired. Only Little Beaver and his father took flight. His mother, Red Dress, remained in the lodge. When almost to the timber, Little Beaver bethought himself of his forgotten gun. He decided to return for it. Scarcely had he secured this treasure and regained cover of the river's bank when troopers raced by.

By this time, his father had disappeared in the timber. Thus separated from him, Little Beaver joined a group consisting of three women, three children and two young bucks making their way toward the lower camps under protection of the high river bank. At one place they found the water to be too deep to be waded in safety. They decided to take a short-cut, even though by so doing they were compelled to cross an open space. They now were nearly a mile below the village and they thought they might escape detection. But they were soon discovered. This was the group toward which Major Elliott and his squad rode when they gave up chase of Magpie and Pushing Bear.

The two young Braves with this group were named Hawk and Blind Bear. Seeing the soldiers coming, Bling Bear said to Hawk:

"Here come soldiers. They will catch us. Maybeso they will kill all. Let us run. The soldiers will see that we are braves and that the others are women and children. Maybeso they will pay no attention to the women and children but will ride after us. While they are chasing us, our friends can run back to the timber and escape."

Hawk accepted the challenge. Immediately they dashed away, running as fast as they could in the deep snow with a frozen crust on top. They ran directly east, toward some high hills beyond which they knew were the camps of the other Indians.

But the soldiers did not give chase immediately. They first rode up to the women and children. Instead of killing them, Elliott detailed Sergeant Major Walter Kennedy to escort them back to Black Kettle's village, there to be turned over to Custer. Then pursuit of Blind Bear and Hawk was begun.

By this time the fleeing youths had put several hundred yards between them and their pursuers. Hope now began to grow in the breasts of these youthful Indian heroes that they might escape the death they had considered certain when they commenced their sacrificial dash. Beyond the next rise, only half a mile distant, lay the camp of the Arapahoes. Should they be able to top this rise before being overtaken, they might escape. Once the immense Arapahoe village and that of the Kiowas were sighted by their pursuers, the soldiers certainly would turn back. So these youths reasoned.

On they pushed. Then hope began to wane as their strength failed. On solid ground they might have won. Deep, crusted snow was a tremendous handicap. Rapidly the horsemen bore down on them. With safety for the staggering youths almost in sight, the troopers drew within range. They opened fire. Down went Blind Bear; then Hawk.[3]

No sooner had the detachment rode after Blind Bear and Hawk than Little Beaver grasped his re-

-----

3. See Appendix J for sequel to the killing of Blind Bear and Hawk.

volver. It was in a holster secreted under his arm. There it had been unobserved by the soldiers. Little Beaver urged the squaws to detract attention of their single guard so that he might get out his gun and shoot the trooper. They then would be free.

The squaws demurred.

'Maybeso the gun is not loaded," objected one. "That would be bad."

Little Beaver was forced to admit he was not certain, but he thought it was loaded. He tried to keep it loaded at all times.

"What if you do not kill the soldier?" wailed another. "Then the soldier will kill us all."

Cautiously, Little Beaver sought to examine the gun. His move was noted by the guard. Kennedy commanded the boy to surrender his arm.

Little Beaver complied.

Then the return to camp was resumed. Herding his charges in front of him, Kennedy continued to ride his horse.

The start west had been made from the east side of a little branch running into the Washita. Prisoners and guard had crossed this creek and were moving up the western slope when one of the squaws chanced to glance toward the river only a short distance away. She saw the figure of a mounted Indian flash past a break in the timber line. He was on the opposite side of the river. Another and still another followed. She knew word of the battle had reached the lower villages and that in a few minutes the valley and hills would be literally alive with warriors rushing to the scene of action.

Oh, for an opportunity to delay her own party! Chance of rescue would be much better if they could be discovered by their friends before reaching the top of the hill, for beyond might be a large number of soldiers.

Suddenly she had an inspiration. The two smal-

lest children were without moccasins. Their feet
were bleeding from contact with the crusted snow
and the brush of the river bank they recently had
left.

Halting, she directed attention of Kennedy to
those bleeding feet, making signs that she wanted to
bind them up. The squaw tore the sleeves from her
dress and began to wrap them around the lacerated
and swollen extremities of the children. She was as
deliberate as she dared to be yet avoid creating suspicion of the alert sergeant major who had them in
his charge. Occasionally she would look up at the
soldier, crooning sympathetically to the children.
Not only did she look at Kennedy; she looked past
him. And what she saw sent a thrill through her
crouched frame. A horseman had dashed out of
the timber and was riding hard for the little group.
Back of him came three others.

It was Little Chief, an Arapahoe, in the lead. The
others were Tossing-up, Lone Killer and Kiowa.

Excitement she could not conceal must have
shown in the squaw's eyes. That or something else
caused Kennedy to turn his head toward the river at
that instant.

Throwing his carbine to his shoulder, the soldier
fired in the general direction of the on-rushing Arapahoes.

Little Chief's rifle blazed reply.

Both shots went wild.

Digging his heels into his horse's sides, Kennedy
headed for Custer's position, attempting to throw a
new shell into his carbine.

Freed from their guard, the Indian women and
children broke for the river, most of them to be
picked up behind warriors who now began to swarm
from the river. They were carried thus to the Arapahoe village of Little Raven.

So intent on his chase had been Major Elliott

and his men that they had failed to notice what was transpiring behind them. Nor had they observed activities in the valley at their left.

By the time Elliott had overtaken and slain the two young braves he and his detachment had been pursuing he heard shots and shouts to his rear. He turned in time to see Kennedy dragged from his horse and killed. He also observed other warriors riding up the valley on both sides of the Washita.

Putting spurs to their tired horses, the troopers set out to retrace their steps. From the first, it was apparent they would have to fight their way back to Custer. The four Arapahoes who had accounted for Kennedy now had been joined by five others and were riding to meet the soldiers. The newcomers were Left Hand, Black Bull, White Bear, Yellow Horse and Two Wings.

Their horses too nearly spent to make a run for it, Elliott decided to dismount his men that their aim might be better. Such were tactics of the cavalry of that day, every fourth trooper leading horses of three other comrades.

Orders were given to dismount, kneel and prepare to fire.

Their fire was withheld until the nine Indians riding down on them divided suddenly. Not a bullet found its mark. Circling, the Indians emptied their rifles at the soldiers, also ineffectively. Then they charged the led horses, hoping to stampede them. A few did break loose.

Loading as they advanced, the soldiers moved forward a few rods and as the red men swooped down upon them again, they discharged another volley. Timing the blast accurately, the Indians threw themselves to the opposite side of their racing ponies. Not one of them was struck.

Alternately halting to deliver a volley at their circling foes and then advancing a short distance while reloading, the beleaguered band moved slowly toward safety.

Before Elliott had covered more than a fraction of the distance to camp at this slow rate of retreat, the numbers of his tantalizing foemen had multiplied many times. Soon Kiowas and Cheyennes, as well as Arapahoes were all around him. This circling horde formed a whirling ring of death which drifted slowly westward. Through it Elliott could not break. Enemy reinforcements now were pouring in with ever increasing rapidity as warriors rode up from the more distant villages.

His progress grew slower and slower. Enveloping ranks of red men became more and more daring as braves vied with each other in riding close to the soldiers.

They reached the ravine in which Kennedy had been killed. Further advance seemed impossible. So far their ranks still were intact, but the last of their horses had been stampeded or slain. Immediately in front of them the branch creek formed a bend to the west. Its banks were precipitous, preventing the Indians charging close from that direction. Tall grasses and weeds made it possible to drop from sight by lying prone on the snow. Here Elliott decided to make a stand. Custer's command was little more than a mile away. Even if the plight of Elliott's men was not yet known to the general, certainly the sound of firing soon would be heard and succor would be sent.

Ordering his men to form themselves in a circle, feet to the center, faces to the foe, Elliott prepared for a courageous defense of that position until rescued.

Soon he was to discover that the very conformation of the stream which had caused him to select this spot for his last stand was proving more of a hazard than a protection. While the banks of the bend prevented horsemen charging his position from that direction, the Indians soon began to dismount and to use these same barriers to shield themselves from sight of the soldiers and their bullets as they maneuvered to within a few feet of the prostrate troopers. From there they could shower the area with arrows, or direct effective rifle fire every time a soldier would raise his head above cover to reconnoiter the situation or to take better aim. Wild grasses and wild sage which screened the troopers from sight of their foes also prevented them seeing their opponents. It was either take chances of hitting their mark by firing in the general direction of the Indians, or risk inviting a burst of bullets and a shower of arrows by rising to their knees.

Minutes passed. Carbines continued to bark. They were answered by the sharper notes of rifles. Occasionally an arm, lifted above cover, popped an ineffective slug aimlessly beyond. Ears were strained to catch the sound of charging cavalry hoofs; but the only hoofbeats audible were those of the swift ponies bringing new reinforcements to the already overwhelming force of red men circling and shouting and shooting.

Carbines barked with less frequency. Rifles rattled faster. Popping of pistols came only from the outer circle, none any longer from the center. The painted, whooping, taunting horde swirled nearer. It seemed to sense the beginning of the end of the struggle.

From the east came a new war whoop. Bursting from a single throat it came nearer and nearer. Down the hillside rode a solitary warrior brandishing above his head an oddly-shaped war club. His pony was lathering from a hard ride, still being urged forward at breakneck speed.

That warrior was Tobacco. The Cheyenne who had headed the avenging circle of Cheyennes and

Sioux which had wiped out Kidder's band above Fort Wallace during Custer's first Indian campaign, was riding to a similar coup.

How long Elliott might have held out but for the arrival of Tobacco is problematical. His enemies had not dared to charge his position up to that time. But Tobacco never hesitated. He had sized up the situation the instant he topped the hill. Immediately he had concluded that his belated arrival called for a rash display of valor. He determined to deliver.

Straight toward the soldier ring he headed. Into it he dashed. Over the prostrate troopers he rode. As he was about to emerge from the opposite side of the circle of doomed men a bullet struck him in the chest. His horse cleared the fatal spot, riderless.

Tobacco's medicine had failed him at last. But his example demanded emulation. There was a concerted rush to follow the trail he had blazed.

Even had Custer come to Elliott's rescue then, he would have been too late.

The fact that not one of those who followed Tobacco was killed or wounded indicates that only a few of Elliott's men still were alive at that time, or that their ammunition had become exhausted.

When Sheridan, Custer, the Seventh regulars and the Kansas volunteers arrived several days later, they found the bodies of Elliott and his men still lying in this circle of dead. The surgeon of the Seventh made a note of the dead and the wounds in each body. His report showed Major Joel H. Elliott, Sergeant-Major Walter Kennedy, three corporals, a ferrier, six privates and three unidentified, a total of fifteen.

Custer's official report immediately after the battle listed "Major Elliott and nineteen enlisted men," a total of twenty, missing.[4] This discrep-

4. See Appendix K.

ancy has led many to believe five of Elliott's followers were killed during the running fight before he decided to make his final stand, though they do not
know how to account for failure of those who buried
the fallen troopers to search for and find the others.
Left Hand said no soldiers were killed except at that
one place. All Indian participants agree that the
only Indian killed here was Tobacco.

There has been considerable speculation, too, as
to the probable length of time Elliott held his foes at
bay, waiting in vain for succor from Custer. Pointing to the overwhelming number of Indians, many
believe this little band was exterminated in short
order, probably too quickly for Custer to have rescued it, even had he known of the plight of these un-
fortunates. Others point to the dearth of casualties
among the Indians as evidence that they waited until the soldiers had nearly exhausted their ammunition before the final charge and that Tobacco happened to arrive about that time to precipitate the finishing thrust.

Since the soldiers went into battle that morning
with at least one hundred rounds of ammunition
each, and, since they appreciated the necessity of
conserving these precious supplies as much as possible, the exchange of shots may have lasted a long
time. There was a pile of empty cartridges near
each dead soldier when their bodies were discovered
later.

Left Hand, who was in the scrimmage from the
time Kennedy was slain until the finish of the last of
Elliott's men, said this fight lasted most of the morning. From the beginning the Indians knew they had
these soldiers at their mercy and eventually would
kill them all. Under such circumstances it was not
customary for Plains warriors to take unnecessary
risks. They aparently were extremely cautious this
time for the soldiers evidently fired at least one

thousand shots, yet killed only one Indian.

But Custer was too interested in events transpiring within the village itself to be concerned with possible disaster to any of his men who should be endangered as a result of their vigorous efforts to round up fugitives. Each lodge was being searched for hiding squaws and papooses, for arms, ammunition, provisions and robes.

Though deeply engrossed in the work of plunder and destruction, Custer could not help but notice the increasing number of warriors making their appearance on the ridges north and south of the village. All were hideously painted, decked out in full war regalia. At the time he had made his spectacular dash into Black Kettle's camp, he believed the three or four hundred slumbering inmates of those lodges inside his converging lines were the only Indians in that vicinity. Before noon, however, so many braves had appeared on the surrounding hills he wondered if it had been possible for that many to escape the net he had laid so carefully. When their numbers continued to increase and they began harassing him on all sides, his early surprise turned to concern.

From a sister of Black Kettle, whom he had captured, he learned that he had stumbled into the greatest concentration of Indians on the Southern Plains.

His concern was heightened by realization that ammunition was running low. Each trooper had been supplied with only one hundred rounds before leaving the wagon train. Promiscuous firing during the first assault had spent many a cartridge from each man's precious supply. Repeated dashes by warriors to the very brink of the plateau at the southern edge of the camp had called for repeated volleys to drive them back.

Now the pressure was increasing on that front.

What if the wagon train bearing reserve supplies

had fallen into the hands of the enemy? It was a harrowing thought.

Suddenly there was commotion on the hills northwest. Down the trail made by Custer's column advancing to the attack, galloped a squad of cavalrymen. Behind them, mules foaming with lather and hubs smoking from friction, bounced a convoy wagon.

"Ammunition!" shouted Quartermaster Bell as he drew rein.

Mules were unhitched in a flash. A score of hands overturned the wagon, spilling ammunition cases into the snow. Other hands threw snow on the smoking hubs.

This desperate ride and timely arrival of supplies, so sorely needed, undoubtedly saved Custer then from the same fate that overtook him eight years later.

Knowing Custer had been following a hot trail intending to attack as soon as he could overtake those he was pursing and, knowing his men had a limited supply of ammunition, the quartermaster had loaded a convoy wagon with these supplies and with a detail of twenty-five troopers he had left the slow moving train to push rapidly ahead, following Custer's well-beaten path. Approaching the scene of action he heard heavy firing. He quickened pace of his six selected mules. Then he sighted the milling red men. Before they had discovered his presence, however, Bell applied the lash and broke through the enemy lines without so much as being fired upon.

Destruction of the village and the captured pony herd yet was to be accomplished. While lodges blazed and huddled, terror-stricken groups of ponies withered before carbines of troopers assigned to their slaughter, the red men resumed harassing the outposts with renewed vigor. Not daring to rush the village for fear of bringing death to those women and

children held captive by Custer, they contented themselves with repeated attempts to draw soldiers out of
their protected position for a test of fighting prowess. They taunted the soldiers as cowards; dared
them to come out and fight. Before Custer made his
charge, he had ordered his men to remove their overcoats and haversacks and leave them in the timber
where they then were halted. These the Indians
had found and had confiscated. Now they waved
these articles as they dashed near the embankment
where the soldiers had sought shelter, challenging
them to come and get them.

But the soldiers would not accept these chal-
lenges. Only when pressure became unbearable did
they strike back. Even then they limited their
counter-attacks to the shortest of sorties. Never did
they trust themselves far enough from the main
body of troops to enable their alert, hard-riding foemen to cut them off and force a decisive battle.

Huge piles of tepees, buffalo robes, buffalo meat,
saddles, bows, arrows and other plunder had been reduced to smoldering embers. The last of eight hundred captured ponies had been shot; that is, all except those appropriated to their own use by soldiers
and those reserved to transport prisoners and such
of the booty as was to be taken back to Camp Supply. The wounded, soldiers and prisoners, had received first aid.

Custer prepared to reform his forces and move
against the lower villages. Encouraged by the ease
with which he had captured Black Kettle's camp, he
believed he would have no serious difficulty completing subjugation of the others.

Ben Clark protested vigorously. He called Custer's attention to the fact that Black Kettle's camp
had been only a small outpost, isolated from the larger villages, that surprise had much to do with Custer's quick triumph there. He warned that, while Cus-

WASHITA BATTLEFIELD TODAY

Above: Black Kettle's village stood in the area now bordered by the railroad.
Below: Sergeant Major Creek where Major Elliott's men were surrounded and killed.

ter's men had outnumbered Black Kettle's warriors by probably five to one, the odds now were with the enemy. Warriors on the surrounding hills and in the villages below likely numbered at least five to each soldier in Custer's command. They were thoroughly aroused, thirsting for vengeance, and eager to draw the soldiers into the open where they could be attacked. He also cautioned Custer that even the additional ammunition which Quartermaster Bell had delivered by his dramatic, death-defying dash through the encircling cordon had been largely expended during the sporadic fighting which had been going on all day. The scout told Custer his contemplated move would be little less than suicide.

Then Clark proceeded to take more of Custer's conceit out of him. He told his chief that it would take strategy—and the aid of Providence—to extricate the soldiers from the dilemma in which they found themselves at that time. Should the Indians become aware of his intention to retreat, they likely would attempt to prevent it. This meant a precarious, running fight. If the red men, while following and fighting, should discover the wagon train which had been left in the vicinity of the Antelope Hills with only a handfull of men to guard it, they easily could drive off the guard and seize all supplies. This would be disastrous.

What do do?

Well, Clark advised, maneuver to give the impression to the watching warriors that he was preparing to set up camp. Horses and men were worn and hungry by the forced march, no sleep and a day of almost constant fighting. Further, such procedure would tend to convince the Indians that the soldiers intended to take their time about future operations. After this respite, men and horses would be in better physical shape for the hardships they were bound to encounter before they could reach Camp

Supply. The Indians would be caught more or less off guard, enhancing prospects of successful execution of the plan, when the return march should be undertaken.

To further disguise actual intentions of the troops, the scout suggested that, when the column should be formed for retreat at dusk, a feint be made as if the soldiers were preparing to move down stream toward the lower camps. He predicted this would cause hasty evacuation of the nearest villages and throw the warriors on the defensive. Then, at the psychological moment, the column could reverse its direction and be well on its way north before the scattered and confused warriors could gather in sufficient numbers to seriously impede its progress.

In spite of his eagerness for further action, Custer finally accepted Clark's plan. Horses and men of the command were fed and rested while strong outposts guarded against any possible attempt at a surprise attack.

At dusk the bugle sounded boots and saddles. The column formed with the band at its head and the prisoners in the center. The band struck up a stirring march. The column headed toward the lower camps. Immediately, alert Indian videttes dashed into the villages to give the alarm.

The ruse was working, just as Ben Clark had predicted.

By now night had fallen. Only the stars overhead and the snow below made it possible for the column to move without confusion. Now was the psychological moment to turn back. Word was passed down the line to counter-march. The column reversed itself. What few Indians were hovering near when this unexpected maneuver was executed were so completely taken by surprise that they had no time to rally a force to attack.

But Custer was taking no chances. He kept the

tired column moving steadily northward until morning. Then he met the wagon train, left behind near the Antelope Hills. Only a brief rest was permitted before the retreat was resumed.

CHAPTER NINE

Clearing the Washita

CUSTER always was a showman, glorying in the spectacular, especially where his own exploits were concerned. Even in a frontier campaign, such as that of the Washita expedition, knowing no one would be encountered except those he considered savages, he began his preparations at Fort Dodge by grouping the horses of his command according to colors. Such organization meant a more attractive display, nothing else. When it came to the actual attack on Black Kettle's village, intended to be a "surprise," he opened the assault with music for which he had brought the regimental band all the way from Camp Supply in spite of the rigors to which he knew these non-combatants must be subjected. The band was playing at the head of his column when it marched away from the smoking battlefield that night.

In keeping with his penchant for dramatic display, Custer began planning how best to set the stage for a reception and demonstration befitting the return of conquering heroes as soon as he had put a safe distance between his rear guard and the menacing mob he had left on the Washita.

He had sent California Joe and Jack Corbin, two of his most dependable white scouts, to General Sheridan with his official report before turning away from the Washita and heading north toward Camp Supply. Arriving at the last camp to be made before reaching his destination, he dispatched another courier to headquarters. This was to suggest to General Sheridan that the commanding officer and staff accord the triumphant regiment then returning from a glorious campaign, a formal review when it should reach headquarters.

The approach to Camp Supply was to be made down a gently sloping plain. As Custer's column neared the crest of the elevation which was to bring it within sight of General Sheridan and staff, he called a halt to arrange his cavalcade in such manner as would present the most imposing spectacle.

His Osage guides were ordered to don their warpaint and take a position with him at the head of the column. Following these were the white scouts. Next came the prisoners; after them the regimental band, the sharpshooters and the troops in regular order. Finally, satisfied with this arrangement, Custer signaled the advance. With Indian scouts shouting their warwhoops and firing their guns, the band playing and colors flying, this pageant moved down the natural outdoor stage and passed in triumphal review before its senior commander and staff.

While the prisoners were being quartered and the soldiers were pitching camp, Custer hastened to report personally to his superior officer.

As Custer's vivid recital reached the missing Major Elliott and fourteen enlisted men, General Sheridan's brow darkened. In a tone entirely different from the flattering voice of a few minutes before, he inquired rather sharply why Custer had left the field of battle without ascertaining the fate of these comrades.

Humbly, Custer sought to justify his action. He explained that the absence of Elliott's detachment had not been discovered until the column was ready to evacuate the village it had destroyed. Then Ben Clark reported having seen the major, followed by a small squad, giving chase to some Indians

BEN CLARK

who had broken through the soldier lines. Elliott, Clark had said, was pursuing them eastward in the direction of the lower camps. Upon receipt of this information, Custer said, he had dispatched searching parties to look for this detachment. The search had extended nearly two miles in the direction the missing men last had been seen, but had proved fruitless.

For a moment Sheridan was silent, lost in grim thought. Then he said:

"Our task has just begun. We must conquer those Indians and put them on their reservations. We must find out what has happened to Major Elliott. I fear the worst. We start as soon as your men and horses are rested."

* * * *

Back on the Washita, other councils were being held. Following Custer's sacking of Black Kettle's village and his sudden, unexpected retreat, those in the other Indian villages wintering in that vicinity knew not what to expect next.

Would the soldiers be satisfied with destruction of Black Kettle's camp, or would they return to attempt the same thing against all others?

If the soldiers proposed to come back, how soon would they return?

If the soldiers did return, would they adjust their differences with the Indians through negotiations, or was this merely the beginning of a new war which would be prolonged indefinitely—until the Southern Plains Indians were exterminated?

Some of the more warlike leaders counseled resistance. They said the Great White Father had broken his promises to the Indians. They proposed going on the warpath. Some of the younger hotheads wanted to attack Fort Cobb as a reprisal. General Hazen had only one troop of cavalry and one company of infantry there as a garrison at that time. The Indians believed this force easily could be beaten and the huge stores of supplies held there could be seized. After all, these supplies belonged to the Indians, they argued.

True, Agent Hazen had been their friend. But why should not the Indians apply the same theory of justice to the Whites as the Whites applied to the Indians? When an Indian anywhere engendered the animosity of the Whites, did not the Whites punish all Indians everywhere they could be found?

With the guns and ammunition which could be obtained by raiding the agency at Fort Cobb, the Indians would be in a position to drive back into Kansas, out of the Indians' country, the soldiers who were there in violation of the Medicine Lodge treaty. They would be in a position to return to their raiding of Texas territory. Now was the time to show the Great White Father in Washington that he could not continue to mistreat the red men who always had yielded to his demands for more and more of their lands. If they did not strike now, they might never again have such an opportunity to assert their strength.

Young braves were not alone in suggesting these actions. Rebellion which had been smoldering in the breasts of their elders threatened to burst forth, to be transformed from thought to demands for action. They could see that if the Government continued to encroach upon their hunting grounds, if soldiers were to be permitted to search out their villages for slaughter, pillage and destruction, there never could be any peace, any security for their families. Why not fight it out to the finish now, rather than be constantly harassed?

Wiser heads prevailed. Even Satanta and Lone Wolf and Satank, leading chiefs of the Kiowas, reversed their first clamor for reprisals. So, too, did Powderface and Left Hand, war chiefs of the Arapahoes, who had led the warriors of Little Raven's band in the attack on Major Elliott's followers, and who had figured prominently in the all-day harassment of Custer's command. They admitted the soldier chief at Fort Cobb (General Hazen) had proved himself to be their friend and should not be punished for offenses of the bad soldier chief (Custer.) To punish the innocent for the guilty was the white man's custom, not that of the red man.

Most of the Kiowas, those of Satanta, Lone Wolf and Satank, and some of the Arapahoes and Comanches decided to move their villages closer to Fort Cobb, where good soldiers would be asked to protect them against the bad soldiers, if Custer's bad soldiers should seek to cause them further trouble.

Others, however, were not so optimistic. Their chiefs were not willing to place their people in further jeopardy by remaining in the path most likely to be taken by invading troops, if, as expected, they should return and seek to treat others as they had dealt with Black Kettle's band.

Kicking Bird led his band to the western extremities of the Wichitas. There, in case of further invasion by soldiers, they either could have the protection of the hills or seek safety in flight to the desert wastes of the Staked Plains. Unless driven to the plains, they could fare better in the mountains. There some protection could be obtained from the wintry winds. There game was more plentiful. There was an abundance of good water. That in the region to the west was not so good. Only a few streams in that gypsum country did not make Indians sick. There they had as neighbors a band of Comanches under Arrow Point, and Woman's Heart's Kiowas.

Others took no chances. They drifted out on the plains northwest of the Wichita range in the vicinity of Sweetwater Creek. These included the Arapahoes of Little Raven, Yellow Bear, Powderface and Left Hand. They included the Cheyennes under the irreconcilable Dog Soldier chief, Medicine Arrow or Stone Forehead, and the Cheyennes of Little Robe.

Satanta and Lone Wolf headed the delegation which went to call upon Hazen. They told him that while the warriors were not afraid to match their prowess against that of the soldiers, they did not want to stir up an enemy which would slaughter women and children and other noncombatants. They said they would rather forego the satisfaction of avenging the deaths of their friends and the invasion of their lands than to see their women and children killed or carried away as slaves by the white soldiers. They asked their white friend for advice.

In asking for advice, they took particular pains to call their agent's attention to the fact that they had done everything within their power to live up to the provisions of the Medicine Lodge peace pact and had waited patiently for the White Father to keep his promises to them. He had promised permanent agency buildings, adequate subsistence and implements with which they could start practicing the white man's mode of living. Although these promises had been made more than a year previously, they had not been fulfilled.

Hazen was greatly perturbed when he heard how Black Kettle had been slain along with the large number of his followers; how Indian women and children had been carried off to captivity and how Black Kettle's camp and ponies had been wantonly destroyed by a ruthless invader. The agent knew this was just the beginning of hostilities. He did not doubt that Custer, reinforced by Sheridan and by the Kansas volunteers, would return for further conquests as soon as he had delivered his prisoners at Camp Supply. There could be little doubt of this, for he knew Sherman and Sheridan had determined upon a well-organized and definite campaign intended to result in absolute subjugation. What already had transpired was only a sample of the slaughter which would result if the Indians knew they would have to fight for their lives and their lands.

Hazen had listened patiently. He was sympathetic. But in his own mind he knew he did not have the power to interfere. Without admitting his helplessness, he tried to reassure his charges. He urged them to go back to their people and wait until he could formulate a plan which might help them.

They departed, unsatisfied, grumbling.

Not only was Hazen now concerned about the safety of the Indians under his jurisdiction, but also for his own safety and that of the staff and small guard of the agency. Were the Indians then near him so minded, it would not be difficult for them to do unto his feeble garrison what Custer already had done to Black Kettle's village. The more he pondered the situation, however, the more he became reassured, insofar as his own safety was concerned. He thought he knew his Indians. He knew that, unlike his white contemporaries in military service on the Plains, the red man did not hold every white man responsible for overt acts of individuals, and he knew they considered him friendly to their cause. Nevertheless, he was greatly relieved a few days later when reinforcements reached him from Fort Arbuckle. He immediately began making preparations for defense of the agency, should trouble break out.

Sending for Satanta and Lone Wolf to come back for another talk, Hazen praised them for their long-suffering patience. He urged them to restrain their young men from any rash attack on the soldiers which might handicap him in his endeavor to pursuade those leading the expected invasion to avoid further bloodshed, should the soldiers come back. He promised them he would get word to the white chiefs, saying the Indians wanted peace, not war; that they were still willing to make any reasonable concessions to insure their safety. He advised Satanta, Lone Wolf and the other chiefs to bring their camps as near to Fort Cobb as convenient so that he might be in a better position to protect them.

Even at the very hour Satanta and Lone Wolf were placing themselves in the hands of the only soldier leader on the whole western frontier who understood their plight and sympathized with them, military propagandists in the East were telling the civilized world these two "bloodthirsty savages" had led the red horde from the villainous clutches of which the marvelous Custer miraculously had extricated his gallant Seventh; that Custer and Sheridan and Colonel Crawford were determined to punish them for their own misdeeds and the misdeeds of those under their leadership.

Indignation over Custer's barbaric raid, however, swept the East as soon as Sheridan's report of the punitive expedition reached Washington.[1] Those correctly informed knew there was no justification for such vicious treatment of these Indians. But that storm of disapproval was too far distant to so much as slacken preparations for "mopping up" along the Washita, which was to be undertaken immediately. This time the invading forces were to be under the direct command of General Sheridan, according to the original plans, but Custer was destined to usurp most of the prerogatives of the leader and to personally direct all contacts with the enemy.

In addition to the Seventh Cavalry and scouts which Custer had with him when he made his first

1. See Appendix L.

thrust, the new expedition included ten companies of the Nineteenth Kansas Volunteer Cavalry, especially recruited for that purpose. This force had reached the rendezvous shortly after Custer had departed on his first scout.

Start of the second drive was made early the morning of December 7. Two thousand men, twice that many horses and mules and three hundred wagons, carrying supplies enough to sustain man and beast for at least thirty days, comprised this, the most pretentious military expeditionary force to see service during the entire conquest of the Southern Plains. It exceeded by six hundred men and, in many other ways, the Hancock Expedition of the previous year which, up to that time, had been by far the most extravagant military gesture of Plains warfare.

First in regular order, moved the augmented company of guides — Indians, halfbreeds, whites. They included such notables as Ben Clark, California Joe, Jack Corbin, Romero, Jack Fitzpatrick, Hard Robe, the Osage, and Neva, the Blackfoot. Behind them came Pepoon's scouts.

Back of the scouts moved the wagon train, wagons four abreast. On the right flank was the Seventh under Custer. On the left plodded the Nineteenth Kansas volunteers under Colonel Crawford, with Lieutenant Colonel Horace L. Moore second in command. This cavalcade swept a path more than a quarter of a mile wide. It was more than a mile and a half from the skirmish line thrown ahead to a similar formation bringing up the rear.

By nightfall this column had covered less than ten miles. It went into camp as soon as it had crossed Wolf Creek. The southern side of this stream was chosen for the bivouac to obtain what shelter might be gained from the timber growing along the banks. The north wind was biting cold.

Three times that distance was covered the next day. The column went into camp that night on Hackberry Creek. It was now within a short march of the South Canadian. This broad river presented a formidable obstacle the third day. It was frozen over. Axes were brought into play to chop a passage near where Custer had crossed the stream two weeks previously on his first invasion.

Thus far, the course had been nearly the same as that Custer had taken before, but, after passing the Antelope Hills, the column was pointed more to the eastward. General Sheridan had determined to strike the Washita as nearly as possible to the scene of the Black Kettle encounter so that he might view Custer's handiwork and try to ascertain the fate of Major Elliott's party.

Up to this time the mystery of their disappearance had remained unsolved. None, however, doubted that these comrades either were dead or were captives of those bands which had chased Custer away from the Washita.

Camping near the scene of previous action, Sheridan assumed leadership of the investigating party. He found Black Kettle's former village much as Custer had left it. Some of the dead bodies of the Indians killed there had been claimed by relatives. They had been carried away or buried. Most of those left behind and uncared for had been furnishing food for wolves, crows, and other scavengers. So had the bodies of nearly eight hundred Indian ponies shot by Custer's orders. They lay strewn over several acres of ground under the bank at the south side of the camp.

Passing from the campsite itself, the searchers were not long discovering evidences that Elliott's men had slain more members of Black Kettle's village than had any of the other four detachments, unless it was Custer's main command which had

charged directly into the village. Fleeing before
Custer's powerful force, hapless villagers who had
sought to make their way through the timber to the
villages below had run into Elliott's deployed squadron sweeping up to meet them. Apparently only
those who had sought protection of the riverbed
escaped, for bodies were strewn thoughout the
woods. Most of them were women and children.
There was evidence that other bodies had been carried away or buried.

Through the woods and over the rise, where Ben
Clark last had seen Elliott chasing some fugitives,
the searching party moved. Then the mystery was
solved—in part. Immediately in front of the scouting line was seen the body of Sergeant Major Kennedy. It had been stripped of its uniform. Closer
examination showed a crushed skull and a body rid-
dled by bullets, bullets most of which had been fired
into the corpse after it had been divested of its
clothing.

Slightly father down the creek, and on the opposite side of it, lay the bodies of the other fourteen.
They, too, had been stripped. Bristling with arrows, they indicated that the Indians had taken no
chance of any being merely wounded. The scene
proved that the victors had vented their vengeance
on the corpses of those comrades Custer had left
to their fate.

Major Elliott's body was prepared for transportation to Fort Arbuckle toward which the expedition
was moving. Those of the enlisted men were buried
after darkness on a knoll on the north side of the
Washita. A single marker, roughly carved by a
member of the Seventh, was placed at the head of
the large common grave.[2]

2. This marker is part of a collection of relics picked
up on the Washita battlefield which are now on display in
the courthouse at Cheyenne, county seat of Roger Mills
County, Oklahoma, where the encounter occurred.

This accomplished, those who comprised the searching detachment returned to the main command. March was resumed. On moved the column past Black Kettle's ruined village to the ground occupied by the other Indian villages below. There property left behind by the Arapahoes, Kiowas, Comanches, Cheyennes and Apaches in their precipitous evacuation was gathered and destroyed.

More bitter grew the weather. Progress became more difficult. Still the caravan pressed forward warily, expecting to come upon the foe at almost any moment. Videts were thrown out on all sides, constantly on the alert lest the expedition run into an ambush. Custer and Sheridan were just as alert for an opportunity to surprise and deal summarily with any enemy camp that might be discovered.

But the Indians were not to be caught napping, either. From the time the expedition had reached the Washita, Indian scouts had kept their chiefs advised of its movement. Consequently, as the column came within a day's march of its destination, runners went flying to Satanta and from Satanta to Hazen, advising of the approach of the soldiers. Satanta and his associates called upon Hazen to do something to prevent these invaders attacking the bands which had placed themselves under protection of their accredited guardian.

Again Hazen informed the protesting chieftains that he had no authority to turn back the expedition nor to issue orders to those leading it. He would, however, expend every possible effort to prevent a fight. He would send word to the commander that all the Indians in the vicinity of Fort Cobb were friendlies. This he did, dispatching couriers to meet the advancing column and deliver to its commander this written message:

LITTLE RAVEN

LONE WOLF

CLEARING THE WASHITA

HEADQUARTERS SOUTHERN INDIAN DIS-
TRICT, FORT COBB, 9 P. M., DECEMBER
16, 1868

TO THE OFFICER COMMANDING
TROOPS IN THE FIELD:

Indians have just brought in word that our troops
today have reached the Washita some twenty miles
above here. I send this to say that all camps this
side of the point reported to have been reached are
friendly, and have not been on the warpath this season. If this reaches you, it would be well to communicate with Satanta or Black Eagle, chiefs of the Kiowas, near where you are, who will readily inform you
of the position of the Cheyennes and Arapahoes, also
of my camp.

Respectfully,

(Signed)   W. B. HAZEN, Brevet Major-
General

While the column was halted to help the wagon
train across one of the many ravines encountered,
the advance guard reported a group of Indians was
approaching under a flag of truce. With the Indians was a white man. The courier also reported
that a large force of warriors was skirting the timber ahead and on the flank, apparently prepared to
attack should their leaders signal them to do so.

With the Osage scout who brought this news
came one of the two runners who had been sent with
Hazen's message.

News that Indians were near spread rapidly
through the command. Especially thrilled were the
Kansas volunteers who were about to encounter
hostiles for the first time. They were eager to see
action, keenly jealous that the regulars already had
participated in one battle.

Advised by the messenger that Satanta was in
a small party of chiefs who had come with him to
consult the soldier leaders, General Sheridan sent
Custer forward to parley. With Custer went other
staff officers, a sizeable bodyguard and interpreters.

It was a three-mile ride before the Indians were

sighted. Custer thanked his lucky stars that he had some fifty of Pepoon's scouts with him, for while the group of chiefs was gathered in the open valley, scores of warriors could be seen in the timber along the river bank. On the hills beyond were hundreds of others.

From the group of chiefs came a signal for a parley. Custer told two of his interpreters to ride forward and meet the two chiefs who already had detached themselves from the others and were galloping forward. Two scouts went to meet them. Their parley was short. Soon the scouts signaled Custer to join them. Taking Colonel Crosby and a few others with him, Custer advanced. As they rode forward, California Joe observed:

"Thar he be! Thar's his ol' satanic majesty hisself, that pompus buzzard there. The biggest of them two heathens aint nobuddy else but Ol' Satanta. An' thet thar tother scalawag alongside uv 'im air Lone Wolf, as yer'll allers find 'em when thar's enny divilment prowlin' round. Take it from a palaverin' galoot who's been a-roamin' 'round these here parts quite a spell, thar'll be narry guarantee thet a civilized human's har'll be sartin' uv stickin' to his think tank this side uv the Platte 'till thet brace uv varmints air put out uv the har-raisin' bizness."

Presently the two groups met.

"How! How!" greeted Satanta, extending his hand to Crosby.

"How! How!" echoed Lone Wolf, addressing Custer.

The profered hands were ignored by both.

Even traditional stolidity of their race could not prevent surprise and resentment flashing into the bronzed countenances of Satanta and Lone Wolf.

"Me Kiowa!" challenged Satanta, striking his chest with clenched fist. Then, apparently deciding that he had not recognized the real soldier chief when he had accosted Crosby, Satanta turned to Custer, again extending his hand.

Again Custer refused to shake hands. Instead, he said through an interpreter:

"I never shake hands with anyone unless I know him to be a friend."

"Me friend," replied Satanta. "Me Kiowa. The Kiowas are friends of their white brothers."

Still Custer remained aloof, haughty. His eyes left those of Satanta for an instant and noted, with some misgivings, the increasing numbers of warriors along the fringe of trees at no great distance.

Satanta appeared to read what was going on in Custer's mind. He knew that at a signal his warriors would come swooping forward and he knew they would prove more than a match for the force Custer had with him.

"Me Kiowa!" again challenged Satanta, once more striking his chest.

Then he softened.

Through an interpreter he told Custer:

"Satanta's young men bring glad news that his soldier brothers have come to visit him. Satanta's heart is glad the Great White Father will now find out that the Kiowas are friends of their white brothers. The white chief Hazen at Fort Cobb send paper talk to his brothers that the Kiowas are friends of the white man. Satanta ride with the runners to tell the strange white soldier chief that he is welcome. The Kiowas have kept the big talk at Medicine Lodge in their hearts and have not been on the warpath. They are waiting for Great White Father at Washington to tell them how to walk the white man's road."

"Seizing messengers sent to me by General Hazen and bringing your warriors to attack my soldiers does not impress me as being the proper way of displaying the friendship you profess," Custer answered. "Where is the other scout who came with this messenger from Hazen?"

"Other white scout with his friends, the Kiowas," returned Satanta. "He will be in our midst in a brief while."

Said Custer:

"If the Kiowas are my friends and if they want to keep out of trouble, let them get away from the bad Indians with whom they have been associated. Let them move in to Fort Cobb where the soldiers can keep bad Indians from inducing them to stay off the white man's road. I have come all the way down here to see that the good Indians stay good and to punish those who refuse to keep off the warpath. I have brought soldiers enough with me to enforce my commands."

Satanta and Lone Wolf assured him nothing would please the Kiowas better; that they merely needed to know what the Great White Father wanted them to do and they would do it. They always had done so. They said they would send messengers to their villages at once to tell their people to move their camps in to Fort Cobb. They asked permission to ride with their new soldier friends on the remainder of their journey.

Such permission was granted.

Considerable disappointment was voiced by the soldiers when they learned there would be no fighting. Amid grumbling protests, the march toward Fort Cobb was resumed. The chiefs rode with Custer while the warriors who had been milling around a few rods distant moved in the same general direction. Runners had been sent to the villages to carry instructions from the chiefs to move to the agency. Both forces kept watchful eyes on each other, determined not to be caught off guard should treachery be attempted.

That night they pitched camps not far apart.

As a special precaution, Custer sent word to the flanking Indians that it would not be safe for them to approach the soldier camp after nightfall lest they be mistaken for hostiles. He also took it upon himself to personally instruct the guards that no prowling Indians were to be permitted inside the lines after dark.

The chiefs, however, were kept in the soldier camp, assigned a spot not far from Custer's headquarters tent. Over them a special guard was mounted.

Supper finished, Custer strolled over to the group of chiefs for a visit. He sought information concerning the location of all the Indian villages, especially those of the fleeing Cheyennes and Arapahoes. These were the bands which had driven him away from the Washita a few weeks previously. They had disappeared while he was on his way back to Camp Supply for reinforcements.

Custer was told they had moved toward the headwaters of Red River, west of the soldiers' present location.

When the general had taken his departure, the chiefs held an informal conference among themselves. Not at all satisfied were they that Custer's mission was one of peace. They feared for the safety of their people if the white soldiers could get them within their power. Was it not a fact that always in the past soldiers had massacred Indian women and children, as well as braves, whenever they had an opportunity?

It finally was decided, however, that all except Satanta and Lone Wolf should go back to their villages and assist in making preparations to come in to Fort Cobb. There General Hazen, their friend, could intercede for them. They would take one more chance of fair dealing. Satanta and Lone

Wolf were to continue to the agency with the soldiers, there to make more definite arrangements concerning disposition and protection of their people.

Next day, after the march once more had been resumed, most of the lesser chiefs rode away from the column to go to their people.

Fearing that Satanta and Lone Wolf might also take a sudden notion to follow suit, Custer threw a guard around them. He informed them that they were his prisoners to be held as hostages to guarantee that his commands were carried out.

Watchful Indian scouts witnessed this seizure from a distance. Convinced by this sudden display of hostility that Custer's mission was far from that he had represented it to be, they hastened to the Indian villages. There they related what had happened. Leaders forthwith determined not to let their people come any nearer the soldiers until they had definite assurance from Hazen, Sheridan and Custer that they would not be harmed.

They asked for a volunteer to go to Fort Cobb to ascertain what kind of treatment was being accorded the two chiefs Custer had so summarily seized, and to find out what progress had been made in negotiations for protection of the Indian bands if they should move in to the agency.

Tsalante, Satanta's oldest son, a stalwart young brave, responded.

He overtook the expedition before it had reached its destination.

From a distance, Tsalante signaled his father to come to him. When Satanta informed Custer of the meaning of the blanket waving all had observed, the general consented to the chief going to converse with his son. But Custer, protected by a strong body-guard, accompanied Satanta.

During the ensuing conference, it was agreed

the youth should ride with them to Fort Cobb, under promise that he would be permitted to go and come at will. He would serve as a courier to the villages as soon as definite plans for locating the Indians could be worked out between Hazen, Sheridan, Custer and the chiefs.

Soon Fort Cobb was reached. Troops established in their more or less permanent camp, Tsalante went back to his people to tell them that Satanta and Lone Wolf were negotiating for a permanent disposition of all the Kiowas. He would keep them advised from time to time of developments.

The terms of Custer and Sheridan as finally determined proved brief—unconditional surrender.

To this, neither Satanta nor Lone Wolf would accede. They wanted assurance of safety and immediate compliance on the part of the Government with the provisions of the Medicine Lodge pact in regard to delivery of supplies and to establishment of a permanent agency. It had been more than a year since the treaty was signed, yet the Government had made no apparent move to keep its promises in these respects.

Followed days of waiting. Neither side would yield.

Sheridan and Custer grew impatient. To their captive chiefs they issued this ultimatum: unconditional surrender of the villages at Fort Cobb by sundown of the following day—or execution of Satanta and Lone Wolf, and pursuit of the villages by the soldiers.

Convinced Sheridan and Custer intended to carry out this threat, unfair though it was, the two chiefs decided to capitulate. Not that they were unwilling to sacrifice their own lives, if their personal sacrifices would have benefited their people, but they did not want another war. They knew their refusal meant bloodshed, the slaughter of innocents and eventual triumph of their enemies.

To the villages hastened Satanta's son with this ultimatum. He also carried instructions from Satanta and Lone Wolf for the Kiowas to come in.

This they did, all except Kicking Bird's village and that of Woman's Heart. These fled west of the Wichitas.

Even then Custer refused to release Satanta and Lone Wolf. He kept them prisoners, manacled in their prison tent, an armed guard always over them lest they escape.

CHAPTER TEN

Putting Custer on the Spot

*N*EARLY two months had passed since organization of the Washita campaign. Troops had been in the field practically that length of time. Largest of the three expeditions directed against the tribes south of the Arkansas had reached its southern goal. Nothing had been heard from the other two.

As their accomplishments, Custer and Sheridan could list:

Assassination of Black Kettle, leading advocate of peace among all the Plains Indians.

The scalps of a dozen of his warrior followers and those of several times that many Indian women and children.

Fifty-three prisoners, all women and children, delivered to Camp Supply.

One small village sacked and burned.

Two unoffending Kiowa chiefs held prisoner through breach of faith, leaders who had surrendered their followers only when it became necessary to do so to escape a possible massacre similar to those of Sand Creek and the Washita.

Proposed crushing of all tribes between the converging columns had failed utterly. By far the greater portion of the intended victims had escaped the army's well-laid plans and now were scattered throughout the wilderness regions to the west. Little Raven's Arapahoes were at large. So were Cheyennes led by Little Robe, Medicine Arrow, Tall Bull, Whirlwind, Bull Bear, Spotted Elk, Heap of Birds, Slim Face, Gray Head and others. Kicking

Bird's Kiowas and those of Woman's Heart still were abroad. So were bands of Cheyennes. All of these had been transformed from friendlies into hostiles by the white man's breach of the Medicine Lodge pact and by this armed invasion of the region set apart for the unrestricted use of these same bands.

The job had been bungled.

It was mid-winter. There was grave doubt that the task to which "generals without jobs" had been assigned could be finished before the greening grasses of spring would make it possible for the angered Indians to sweep north into white settlements again with devasting raids of retaliation. At least there would be need of a permanent military post of no small proportions in that region from which troops could operate from Red River to the Arkansas. It might take years to conquer the Southern Plains. Fort Cobb, the present base of operations, was not suitable for such a pretentious base.

Selection of a site became General Sheridan's objective while General Custer sought to locate various large bands of Indians which had escaped him. He proposed to force them on to restricted areas where troops could keep them under subjection always.

From Indians who came to Fort Cobb for supplies, Sheridan and Custer learned there was an area just east of the Wichita Mountains which might prove to be a desirable location for the new post. There Medicine Bluff Creek flowed along the northeastern foot of the mountains before turning south to empty into a never-failing sweet water tributary of Red River. There was to be found an ample supply of stone and timber for construction of the contemplated fort. Outside the mountains, the ground was level, the soil rich.

Early in January the change in location was ordered. Horses of the Kansas volunteers had been taken from them soon after their arrival at Fort Cobb and had been sent to Fort Arbuckle. The volunteers had been turned into foot soldiers. Accompanied by many hardships, the transfer was made. The Kansans established their camp near where Slough Creek empties into Cache Creek. The Seventh Cavalry set up two miles father down. Beyond the location of the Seventh's camp, General Sheridan selected the site for a permanent post.

So came into being Fort Sill. Members of the Seventh suggested the new post be named for Major Elliott, but Sheridan chose the name of Sill in honor of Joshua W. Sill, a classmate of his at West Point, who had fallen in the Civil War battle of Stone Mountain. With the establishment of Fort Sill came the passing of Fort Cobb as a military post.

While Sheridan builded and Custer attempted to communicate with recalcitrant Indian bands, members of the two regiments hunted wild game in the mountains and amused themselves in and about camp, each to his own liking.

Arrival of a portion of the Evans column from Fort Bascom, New Mexico, brought information that most of the Indians Custer was seeking were west and northwest of the Wichitas. The column had encountered Horseback's small village of Comanches and had engaged its warriors, led by Arrow Point, in a Christmas day skirmish opposite the mouth of Devil's Canyon. Some of Woman's Heart's Kiowas also had participated in the closing scenes of this scrimmage, indicating that several bands were encamped not far away.

Friendly Indians Custer had enlisted as mediaries confirmed this information. Particularly was Custer interested in the report that Little Raven's

Arapahoes, those under Yellow Bear, Medicine Arrow's Cheyennes and those of Little Robe were spending the winter near the source of Red River in the vicinity of the Palo Duro.

Little Raven, Custer was advised, had become separated from the main force of Arapahoes. He had only sixty lodges with him.

While still doubtful of the motives which prompted Custer to pursue them so relentlessly, both Little Robe of the Cheyennes and Little Raven of the Arapahoes expressed a willingness to negotiate. They sent word to Custer that Little Robe and Yellow Bear, second chief of the Arapahoes, would pay Custer a visit to see what could be done to prevent further trouble.

Appreciating the disadvantage he would be under, should he attempt to resort to force of arms in that desert region, Custer went to extremes in his pledges of friendship and good will toward all bands which voluntarily came in. At the same time, he threatened severe castigation if compelled to use force.

The two chiefs assured Custer that, although their followers would yield to such terms, their travel necessarily would be slow, due to the weakened condition of their ponies at that time of year. As time went by and they failed to appear, Custer took a small detachment with him and, accompanied by Little Robe and Yellow Bear, set out in search of the villages to see if their departure could not be expedited. They first located Little Raven's village along Mulberry Creek. After an extended conference with the chiefs, of whom Little Raven was the spokesman, Custer prevailed upon the Arapahoes to strike camp and set out for Fort Sill.

The Cheyennes, Little Robe advised, were farther out on the Staked Plains. Thither Little Robe departed, while the soldiers remained behind to await needed supplies.

Custer did not dare to follow, even after his supplies arrived, because of the small number of men he had with him. He had the choice of permitting the Cheyennes to elude him entirely or returning with troops and supplies sufficient to enable him to catch them and bring them in by force.

His pride would not permit him to give up. He would return with a force vastly superior in numbers to the fighting effectives of the Cheyennes and compel them to bend the knee to him.

By this time construction of Fort Sill was nearly finished. The Tenth Cavalry, a Negro regiment, had been installed as its garrison. Seeing no need of his further presence there, Sheridan determined to return to Camp Supply. Colonel Crawford turned leadership of the Kansas volunteers over to Lieutenant Colonel Moore and went north with Sheridan. They took with them only a few troopers and a number of Pepoon's scouts.

By the first of March, Custer was ready for his final smash. On the second he set forth. It was to be a long march and a slow one, for the Kansans were without mounts. The best that could be done under the circumstances was to transport all their equipment, except the clothes they had on, in the wagons. Overcoats, haversacks and sometimes guns were consigned to these vehicles.

His line of march carried Custer along the south side of the Wichita Mountain range, past old Camp Radziminski, across the North Fork of Red River and the Salt Fork to Gypsum Creek. Here part of the wagon train and many of the footsore infantrymen were sent north along the Texas line to go into camp on the Washita near the ruins of Black Kettle's village. There they were to await arrival of the remainder of the expedition. The others continued west.

Next day an Indian trail was discovered.[1] It was a small trail in the beginning, broadening as it progressed. Apparently it had been made by bands out hunting which had come together, one by one, until the broadening path indicated a sizeable force was ahead. It led the expedition several miles beyond the source of the Salt Fork, turned north and bore slightly to the east. Projected far enough and continued in the same direction, it would lead back to the Washita at a point not far from the region from which Custer had dislodged some of these same Indians three months previously.

Nearly three weeks after setting out from Fort Still, Custer finally came upon the object of his search. There along the Sweetwater were the last free remnants of the Southern Cheyennes. Nearest to him was the small group of lodges inhabited by Little Robe. Farther up stream, five times as large as Little Robe's cluster, was the main vil-

---

1. In his "Campaigning with Custer," page 142, David L. Spotts, a member of the Nineteenth Kansas Volunteer Cavalry, tells this amusing occurrence incident to striking this first trail and the small camp to which it led:

"Monday, March 8, 1869. Early this afternoon the scouts came back and reported an Indian camp in advance. It was raining pretty hard, but we were carrying our guns under our coats so the water could not get in the magazines and wet the cartridges. We were told to halt while the cavalry made the attack. We stood in the rain until the 'battle' was over, and then were ordered to advance and go into camp near that of the Indians. It was then we heard about the 'attack.' There were eight Indians and one squaw in the party. The Indians (men) had apparently not returned from the hunt and the squaw had the meal on the fire when the Seventh came in sight. She left everything, jumped on a pony and started for the left side of a circular piece of timber to the right. General Custer took the other side of the timber, expecting to head her off, but she never came that way, but went up a small ravine to her left and upon the plains. By the time her trail was found she was out of sight and miles away, for they never saw her any more."

Spotts adds that the Kansans had a great deal of enjoyment out of kidding the Seventh about being unable to capture even a single squaw.

lage of Medicine Arrow. It was a powerful village, containing the bravest, boldest, and most accomplished warriors on the Plains. They were the unquenchable spirits of the Cheyennes, convinced of the righteousness of their cause and consecrated to upholding the traditions of their once great nation.

This attitude was due partly to faithfulness to their trust, partly to their belief in protective powers of the Sacred Arrows of the Cheyennes with which this band had been entrusted. For generations— ever since this supreme medicine had been given the Cheyennes by their Culture Hero—it had been part of the tradition which came to them with these shafts that evil would overtake the nation if these omens should pass into possession of the enemy. Should this band surrender, bringing the arrows even into indirect possession of their white enemies, and should disaster befall his people after that, Medicine Arrow would feel that he had been responsible for their misfortunes.

On the other hand, tradition assured the Cheyennes that their nation could not be conquered so long as the medicine of the arrows was not violated. Past performances seemed to justify this belief in protective powers of these talismen.

Immediately after assassination of Black Kettle and destruction of his village, members of Medicine Arrow's band had lost no time putting as much distance as possible between themselves and the soldiers. They had headed for the last sanctuary known to them, a sanctuary considered proof against white man's aggression, not through any treaty, but because of nature's barrier—the Llano Estacado or Staked Plains. Hither they did not believe the soldiers would dare to follow them. Only those enured to terrible hardships and possessing knowledge of every hazard and oasis were believed capable of existing out there.

It meant hardships and suffering during the winter when game is scarce and blizzards sweep with relentless fury across barren, trackless wastes that offer few obstructions to their pitiless pounding. It meant more hardships and more suffering during the blistering summer, when blazing suns burn everything to a crisp and hot winds drive sands of the desert with stinging force. Perhaps time would cause the Great White Father to be less drastic in his demands, might cause him to keep his talk straight for once. Then the last of the Cheyennes could return to their paradise along the Washita. But, if not, better to be free Cheyennes, true to sacred traditions of their people, faithful to the Sacred Arrows, even though forced to endure extreme adversity, rather than become slaves of a faithless enemy.

Little Raven, too, had lost faith in the word of the white man. He who long had been a champion of peace, the most eloquent of all those who had pleaded the causes of the red man in every important peace council, finally had come to the conclusion that the Great White Father was determined to exterminate the Plains tribes if he could. The Washita Massacre had turned abiding faith into absolute distrust. So he, also, had gone to the Staked Plains with his allies, the last of the Cheyennes.

But now, Little Raven, too, had been talked into yielding once more. Still, on Little Raven's shoulders rested no such heavy responsibility as the sanctity and safety of the sacred shafts. Nor were the spirits of the Arapahoes as intractable as were those of the Cheyennes.

Yes, Little Raven might, with impunity, give in once more to the soft words of the Great White Father's emissaries. Not so Medicine Arrow! Not so the last of the Cheyennes!

Medicine Arrow had selected for his isolated retreat an ideal location on the only sweet water stream in that region of brackish creeks and rivers. Trees grew thickly. Grasses managed to exist along its limited valley. It was a blessed oasis. Here were trees for fuel in winter and shade in summer. Elevations on either side provided a certain amount of security and snugness for the village. Here was a sufficiency of cottonwood sprouts and rugged shrubs to sustain their horses until spring should bring on greening grasses. Furthermore, only a few miles of a gentle divide intervened between this new haven and the headwaters of their beloved Washita. There they might return in the spring when their ponies should regain their strength, even though such a visit should necessitate the greatest of stealth.

Along this creek the three hundred lodges of Medicine Arrow's followers were pitched. Hunting parties had managed to supply the camp with food sufficient to carry its inhabitants through the remainder of the winter.

Hope that his people might remain there undisturbed was shattered when Medicine Arrow learned from Little Robe that Custer was defying the elements to hunt them out. From that time on, constant watch was kept for the approach of expected troops. They had arrived at last.

Definite plans had been made far in advance by Medicine Arrow. If Custer insisted upon war, the village was under instructions to break up at a minute's notice and scatter so that successful pursuit would be impossible. Warriors would cover the retreat. If the white chief came upon a peaceful errand and would talk straight, Medicine Arrow and his chiefs and headmen would determine their course of action according to developments of the proposed big talk.

Medicine Arrow proposed to take no chances of

being destroyed by the man whom he had very good reasons to mistrust. The supreme power of the Medicine Arrows would be invoked to protect the red man against any further treachery on the part of this white persecutor. The proposed big talk would be made in the Arrow Lodge. Custer would be put through the arrow ceremony, last word in Cheyenne necromancy.

The stage had been set for this rite before Custer, riding ahead of the main body of troops with a sizeable bodyguard, neared the waiting village.

Courteously but rather imperiously, Medicine Arrow and his associates greeted their visitor. Welcome was extended and hope was expressed that the visit was one of friendship. No sooner had these formalities been exchanged than Custer and an officer or two were escorted to the Arrow Lodge for a formal conference. Only Custer was invited to enter. The others were extended hospitality in an adjacent tepee.

As the chiefs, other Cheyenne dignitaries and Custer disappeared within, a solitary horseman stood watch a few paces from the slitted entrance. Long legs, neatly encased in semitight-fitting buckskin leggins, dropped moccasined feet well below the body of the spotted pony upon which he sat. A loose-fitting jacket of skins was caught about a slender waist by a heavy-buckled belt. From this belt protuded the butt of a pistol of rather ancient design. Alongside was a keen, long-bladed hunting knife. Across shoulders, already beginning to broaden with vigorous manhood, was slung an unstrung bow, made from the wood of the bois d'arc and an unadorned quiver of steel-tipped arrows. The glossy, black hair of his uncovered head was caught in twin braids. Entwined with flannel ribbons of brilliant crimson and green, they reached well down his arrow-straight back. No saddle or blanket cushioned

his seat on the back of his spirited mount. Sole item
of riding equipment was a short lariat tied loosely to
the under jaw of the pony after a fashion typical of
Plains Indians.

Repeatedly, the youthful, self-appointed sentinel
shifted his gaze from the ridge in the south to the
doorway of the lodge in front of him.

He had been alongside his father, Big Man, half
an hour previously when they had ridden forth with
Medicine Arrow to meet Custer. He also had been
with his father less than five years before, when they
rode into the shambles on Sand Creek. He had raced
afoot alongside his father as they fled from their
lodge on the banks of the Washita that cold November morning just four months ago when Custer began sacking Black Kettle's peaceful village. The
wound where a bullet fired by one of Custer's men
had pierced his leg still was tender reminder of that
conflict.

It was while listening to Custer's protestations
of friendship and peaceable intentions a few minutes
previously that young Magpie had determined to do
his part should treachery once more be attempted
by the white soldier chief.

Thus determined, he had ridden to his father's
tepee while the criers were calling the various chiefs
of the village to council. There he had armed himself. He had arrived at his post just as the last of
the tribal leaders was lifting the flap of the lodge to
enter. He was close enough to the doorway to enable him to catch a glimpse of the assemblage
within.

Directly opposite the entrance to this magnificent temple of laced and ornamented buffalo hides,
loomed the imposing figure of Medicine Arrow,
decked in full ceremonial regalia. On either side
ranged other members of this silent, solemn circle.
All were seated cross-legged on buffalo robes on an

earthern floor as tidy as the polished oak of a king's palace. In the center smoldered a fire. Even as the last counsellor entered, Medicine Arrow's squaw had followed to toss upon these embers an armload of fuel. Immediately it burst into a cheerful blaze. This task accomplished, she glided out, dropping the curtain across the entrance to seal the interior of the lodge against outside eyes once more.

But, in that second flash of the interior, Magpie glimpsed the flame-illuminated visage of Custer. The white chief occupied the seat of honor at Medicine Arrow's right. Whether out of deference to the solemnity of the occasion or for comfort, the visitor had removed his black, broad-brimmed campaign hat. It lay on the ground in front of crossed legs which were encased in tight-fitting cavalry boots, reaching well above the knees. From a high, full forehead, long, wavy, yellow hair was brushed back to fall in graceful undulations down the back of his neck and down to his shoulders.

Deep creases separated heavy brows, shading sharp, alert eyes. Slightly sunken cheeks attested the strain of a long, hazardous, eventful campaign and accentuated high cheek bones. A tightly drawn mouth was only partially concealed by a drooping moustache.

Stealthily, Custer surveyed his surroundings.

Statuesque figure of this young brave and his pony, the silence within the Arrow Lodge were in striking contrast to the animated scenes elsewhere in the village. On every hand stern warriors, excited young men and mere boys were dashing madly about. They would gallop to the crest of a ridge to the southward, whence they could observe approach of the soldiers, then race back at top speed to report what they had seen to groups of those who had remained in the village. Children scampered everywhere. Squaws were hurrying to the pony herd which boys had driven into the camp. Selecting pack horses, they were dragging them back to their respective lodges. Everything was being placed in readiness to strike camp and scatter, should negotiations then being conducted between the great white chief and their own leaders in the Arrow Lodge fail to protect them from attack by that long column of troops couriers had reported approaching from the south.

Sensing the unusual in this sudden stir, hundreds of dogs of every description raced at the heels of the ponies or chased one another noisily from tepee to tepee. Their sharp barkings added materially to the confusion.

Well might this be considered an occasion warranting the service of the Sacred Arrows. Here was the final refuge of the last pretentious remnant of that picturesque, nomadic legion which, until a few short years before, had roamed the Western Plains at will, from the Black Hills to Red River. This region they had considered their God-given heritage wherein to enjoy life, liberty and the pursuit of happiness. This freedom they had known to the fullest extent until covetous white men sought to drive them from the lands of their fathers. Inch by inch they had yielded, stubbornly contesting the advance of these alien usurpers who treated every treaty with the Indians as a mere scrap of paper to be used to touch off new frontier conflicts.

They had yielded under protest, always seeking to avoid bloodshed, if possible. But they could surrender no further domain and yet continue to live the kind of a life they desired. All their traditions would become mere memories. Even now, were this village permitted to go unmolested, if its inhabitants could continue to roam and to hunt over the territory alloted to them by the Medicine Lodge treaty, theirs would be a precarious existence. Still, they were willing to take their chances rather than submit to what they considered virtual slavery.

Complete silence reigned inside for a minute or two after Medicine Arrow's squaw had taken her departure from the council lodge. Then came a slight rustling of porcupine quills. Magpie knew the medicine man was removing from the folds of his ornate medicine bag a large pipe and ingredients for the contemplated smoke.

While these herbs were being mixed and placed in the bowl of the pipe, the medicine man called upon the Great Spirit to witness that his children, the Cheyennes, were about to smoke the peace pipe with the soldier chief who had come to them from the Great White Father. The Great Spirit was reminded that the Cheyennes always had endeavored to remain at peace with their white-faced brothers, believing it to be his wish. Never had they violated any of the promises made the Great White Father. On the other hand, the white men repeatedly had broken their solemn promises to the red man, causing the Cheyennes to believe white hearts were bad toward them and white tongues were prone to talk crooked.

The Great Spirit was called upon to witness that the brave warriors of the Cheyennes did not fear to try conclusions with those the Great White Father had sent against them. Never had the soldiers been able to conquer Cheyenne warriors in any engagement, but these warriors wished to avoid bloodshed because the Great White Father's soldiers killed women and children and old men. The Great Spirit was assured it was to save the lives of these defenseless innocents that Cheyenne braves were willing to quit the war path against the white man. They were about to smoke the peace pipe once more with the white soldier chief who had assured them the Great White Father would treat the Cheyennes as he would promise. If the white soldier chief again should exhibit a bad heart toward them or violate the promises about to be made, the Great Spirit was asked to forgive his chosen children, the Cheyennes, and ride with them, should they be compelled to take the warpath once more, never again to quit it so long as a warrior was left to carry on.

Came a pause. Medicine Arrow laid aside the pipe and seized Custer's right hand in his left. Pressing clasped hands over his heart, the chief again addressed himself to the Great Spirit. Throughout this part of the ceremony, assembled Indian leaders mumbled responses, each assuring the Great Spirit his heart was good toward his white brother. Should the white brother prove of bad heart, however, each pledged himself never to cease fighting for the rights of the red man so long as they breathed and their hearts kept beating.

Custer's hand was released. The medicine man pointed the stem of the pipe to the four points of the compass. Then he presented it to the Sacred Arrows. His voice called upon these magic shafts to exert their powerful medicine upon the heart of his white brother. Should the soldier leader harm the red man again, the arrows were implored to assist the Cheyennes in avenging all wrongs.

Another pause. The stem was placed between Custer's lips. Again came the modulated chant of Medicine Arrow.

Ordinarily, the peace pipe, once lighted, is passed from mouth to mouth after only a puff or two by each communicant. Not so in the Medicine Arrow ceremony. Signs informed Custer that he was to smoke the entire bowl by himself. When he had finished, Medicine Arrow drew a pipe-stick from his beaded bag. With it he loosened the ashes thoroughly and sprinkled them over Custer's boots. There was an ominous inflection to the concluding words:

"Thus will the Great Spirit destroy the White Soldier Chief if ever he walks contrary to the peace pipe again."

Again the pipe was filled and lighted. This time it was passed around the entire circle of chiefs. Each consecrated himself to peace with the white man, if the white man should deal justly with the Cheyennes.

The ceremony completed, they were ready to discuss the matter which had brought Custer to the Sweetwater. The general told them that all other Indians had come to a realization that further resistance was useless, that the Great White Father had a soldier for every tree on the Plains and, if necessary, he would send all of them out to force the Indians on to reservations.

2. Custer's "Life on the Plains," page 309, describes in detail what transpired within the Sacred Arrow tent, but apparently Custer attached no special importance to the ceremony. The writer obtained the story of its special significance by chance. During one of his visits with Magpie in 1930, he inquired whether the Indians placed any dependence in the word of Custer.

"No," he answered. "That is why they put him through the Arrow Ceremony and emptied the ashes of the pipe on his boots."

"What was the significance of the ashes?" he was asked.

"It made the peace pipe stronger. They had smoked the peace pipe with Custer before and he had broken his word to deal justly with the Indians. The Arrow Ceremony in which Custer was compelled to smoke the entire pipe of tobacco and then the ashes were emptied on his boots meant that if he went contrary to the pipe again (broke faith with the Indians) he would be destroyed like ashes."

Custer went contrary to the peace pipe that very same day when he seized hostages, and the Indians did not trust him again after that. The Cheyennes think the curse of the Arrows followed Custer and was responsible for his death on the Little Big Horn.

Magpie said he sat outside the tent on his pony while this ceremony was being performed, that he helped entertain Custer and also was on the ridge looking back at the soldier camp when Custer attempted to seize the chiefs that same afternoon.

Custer told him he had gone to great trouble to search out Medicine Arrow's village and make arrangements for him to bring his people in to the reservation set aside for them at Camp Supply. He hoped they would be reasonable; that they would go with him without compelling him to use force. Otherwise—well, Medicine Arrow and his friends could see he had brought along enough soldiers to enforce his demands.

Long they conferred. Eventually, Custer was informed the chiefs would call all headmen of the tribe together for a big talk. They promised to let him know their decision as soon as it should be reached.

CHAPTER ELEVEN

Custer Breaks Faith

HE conference ended, the conferees emerged from the Medicine Arrow Lodge. Medicine Arrow accompanied Custer and Cook to point out a suitable place for the soldiers to camp.

Soon camp was being made less than a mile from the village while groups looked on with mingled curiosity and misgivings.

"Medicine Arrow wise chief," Magpie remarked to his father as they watched the soldiers establish themselves for an indefinite stay. "Soldiers no can see Cheyenne village from where they camp."

He spoke truly, for an intervening ridge obstructed the view of one encampment from the other.

"Come," said Big Man. "We go back to the village. Maybeso Medicine Arrow wants to talk to headmen of the bands."

Halfway down the slope that led to the Indian encampment the two encountered Medicine Arrow and a small group of followers riding slowly homeward.

"Medicine Arrow does not trust the soldier chief," Big Man asserted as if reading his superior's mind.

The head chief grunted assent.

"Remember Sand Creek. Remember Pawnee Fork. Remember Washita. It is not good for soldiers to be close to Indian village. Soldiers see all Indians alike—squaws, papooses, old men, braves."

They rode in silence a few paces. Then Medicine Arrow spoke again:

"Medicine Arrow not like way soldier chief smoke peace pipe in Arrow Lodge. Soldier chief smoke pipe with mouth. Eyes show heart not right toward Cheyennes. Hands say he nervous. Want to point gun at Indians; pull trigger. When sun go down and soldiers sleep, village move so soldiers not be tempted. Not too far. More talk with soldier chiefs must be made; maybeso two, three, four sleeps."

Having voiced these observations, he commanded:

"Say to women, 'be ready.' Say to boys, 'cut more limbs for ponies to eat.' Do not hurry. Sun he yet long way to go."

As the group disintegrated, each heading for his particular lodge to broadcast Medicine Arrow's orders, the chief accosted Magpie.

The boy reined in his pony and rode alongside his leader.

Said the chief:

"Medicine Arrow see Magpie by council lodge. Magpie's heart is bitter toward Custer and the soldiers. Maybeso Magpie's leg still tell him where soldier bullet go through. Maybeso Magpie grieve for his kinsman, Black Kettle. Maybeso Magpie want big fight so can kill soldiers and get revenge."

They rode in silence for a moment, the chief pondering his next words, the boy waiting for revelations of an assignment he sensed was coming.

Medicine Arrow resumed:

"Magpie's heart is the heart of a great Cheyenne warrior. His heart beats strong. Maybeso Magpie be big chief when Medicine Arrow is old man and no can fight more. Great warriors fight with heads same as hands. Fight with head, save hands, maybeso save scalp. Magpie fight soldiers better with head now than with bow and arrow or gun or knife. Maybeso save scalp of women and children and old men of village. Save heap lots ponies. Medicine Arrow know Magpie will do what is told him to do."

The boy grunted assent.

Thereupon the chief revealed his next strategy. Magpie was to join in a riding exhibition to hold Custer's attention and that of the soldiers, while the village quietly completed its arrangements for a night move to a point several miles up stream. There it would be in a better position for defense, should the soldiers attack, as Medicine Arrow suspected they might be planning.

Back in the military encampment another conference was in session. With Custer, in his headquarters tent, was Colonel Cook, Dr. Lippincot, Romero and Hard Robe, head Osage scout. A courier had been sent to summon Little Robe.

"I tell you we should have struck the minute we reached the village," Cook was complaining.

"If we had," Custer rejoined, "some villainous squaw would have sunk her knife into the hearts of those captive white women at the first volley. Wait until we get possession of these women. We can settle with Medicine Arrow and his rascals after that. They can't get away from us. Their ponies are in no condition to travel at this season of the year, and we outnumber their effectives at least two or three to one. We have them right where we want them. But we must get those girls first."

He spoke of two white women the Indians had admitted were in their village.

For several minutes they discussed various plans for obtaining possession of the captives before attempting to use duress in forcing the Indians to go with them to Camp Supply.

"If I could get old Medicine Arrow and another or two of the leading chiefs in my hands, without precipitating a general engagement, I could make them come to time like I did with Satanta and Lone Wolf," Custer suggested.

"The old fox is too wary to be caught off guard that way," Dr. Lippincot remarked.

"What do you think, Romero?"

The Mexican scout, interpreter and counsellor, discharged a mouthful of tobacco juice, the better to be prepared for exploiting his wisdom. Said he:

"Medicine Arrow ain't nobody's fool. Yer can whale me for a lop-eared jackass if that red rascal a'int up to one uv his murderin' tricks right this very minute. I calculate he larned from thet thar Little Robe critter that yer air wise to his holdin' them white gals. He has been playin' plenty smart ever since we hove into sight uv his layout. The way he dragged yer off to thet thar tent uv hisn without giving yer time to say 'scat' tells me he air movin' right along with some pre-concocted scheme to deal 'round yer, whatsomever it may be. Thet there outfit uv hisn air all set to light out for the wide open places an' leaven' yer to twiddle yer thumbs the very fust time yer crook yer finger or look like yer gunnin' fer trouble. I takes in the situation potterin' aroun' on top of thet ridge while yer was a-palaverin' in ol' Medicine Arrow's tent."

"All the more reason I should get my hands on some good hostages," Custer rejoined. "But they can't go far. Their ponies can't stand a long march after existing all winter on nothing but the barks and twigs of cottonwoods. My men soon could overtake them. Let them try it. I'll teach them a lesson they will not soon forget."

"What do you think, Hard Robe?" Custer inquired of his Osage scout.

"Cheyenne go this way, that way, every way. Cheyenne know this evil country where to hide, where to find water that does not make him sick. Soldier not know which way to go. Maybeso not find Cheyenne. Maybeso not find water. Maybeso not find game. Maybeso get lost. Maybeso die."

Silence ensued.

"I must have hostages! I must have Medicine Arrow if I can possibly inveigle him into my grasp!" Custer fairly shouted, emphasizing his remarks by slapping his booted knee as he rose from a hardtack box which served for a camp stool.

Fate seemed to be playing into Custer's hands, for even as he got to his feet, an orderly entered to report that Medicine Arrow was without, craving speech with him.

Followed by his associates, Custer stepped outside.

Medicine Arrow greeted him cordially. He informed him some of the young men of the village had come to entertain their distinguished guests with music and exhibitions of horsemanship.

Custer's quick eye appraised the strength of the visiting contingent. He assured Medicine Arrow he felt greatly honored by this splendid display of friendship. Turning to his aides and addressing them in an undertone, Custer ordered them to summon a hundred or more of the best men of the command, instructing them to drift casually and unostentatiously into the circle of spectators but to come fully armed with side arms. When the word was given, they were to seize the principal chiefs to be held as hostages.

Medicine Arrow was among those named as the most desirable. The soldiers were to be cautioned not to fire except in extremity, lest a pitched battle be precipitated. Custer had noted that none of the Indians carried rifles, although the ever-present pistol and hunting knife protruded from many a girdle and a few carried bows and arrows. He noted with satisfaction, also, that none of these bows were strung.

Custer chuckled inwardly as the thought of the consternation and chagrin of Medicine Arrow when that worthy should discover how easily he had been outwitted.

Dismounting from their ponies and, turning over the short lariats which served both as tie ropes and bridles, to boys, the warriors joined Custer and his officers around the blazing campfire as the entertainers began their program.

Only a few warriors were there, most of the small party of Indians inside the circle being boys and young men, Custer observed with keen satisfaction. Some of the older men would not prove formidable antagonists, should trouble result. But they would make good hostages. Truly fortune favored Custer, for scores of his soldiers had come up, completely surrounding the little group and outnumbering the Indians, boys, old men and all, perhaps three to one.

Their performance finished, the entertainers rode off at top speed to disappear over the rise in the direction of the village. After a short dash in that direction, Magpie wheeled his horse and headed back for the group of dignitaries. There were misgivings in his heart. The chiefs had risen, one or two had mounted and the others were preparing to follow suit.

This was Custer's opportunity. At his shouted command, the soldiers drew arms and surrounded their guests.

One reached for Medicine Arrow's bridle as this chief vaulted to the back of his pony. The grasping hand was struck down. A cry of rage and warning, a jerk on the bridle, a dig of heels into the pony's flanks and the startled horse plunged through the cordon of soldiers. Pandemonium reigned. There were shouts, curses and commands, the thudding of hoofs, a short, sharp struggle—but not a shot was fired.

When the scrimmage had ended, Custer found

himself in possession of few prisoners worthy of being retained as hostages. Most of the important chiefs desired had effected their escape. By far the greater portion of those captured were boys and young men. These were permitted to go their way. Only four of the elders were held.

Well might Custer be disappointed at his luck. Instead of Medicine Arrow and other celebrities he had desired, he held a quartet of inconsequential prisoners. One of them was eighty years old, another a cripple. What if the Cheyennes did not consider these hostages of sufficient importance to exchange their two white prisoners for them? He might not be able to make the hostage medicine work against these Cheyennes as he had against the Kiowas a short time previously, when he had held the great Satanta and the mighty Lone Wolf captives under threat of death if his demands were not met.

Consternation, riotous struggle between rage and fear, reckless impulse and sane caution swept the village with tempestuous fury as those who had escaped Custer's treacherous trap raced madly into camp. News of brewing trouble already had preceded them, borne by those who, from the intervening hilltop, had witness the seizures.

Young men, eager for action, galloped wildly about, brandishing weapons and demanding immediate attack. Knowing that all Indians looked alike to Custer's men, when blood lust held sway, squaws were hastening departure of the village. Pack horses had been rounded up earlier in the day when the soldiers first had put in an appearance, ready for any eventuality. Anticipating a night move anyway, many lodges already had been struck. Many a travois loaded with personal effects and with youngsters or old men and old women, too feeble to ride horseback or to trudge alongside. In an unbelievable brief space of time the hegira was on.

Had Custer's scouts topped the ridge between the two rival camps an hour after his ill-starred efforts to seize the head chief, they would have seen the entire village moving rapidly in the opposite direction. Far in the distance they would have seen the straggling equipage with warriors, prepared for action, covering the rear. Calmer heads, including that of Medicine Arrow, had prevailed upon those warriors seeking reckless revenge to consider the safety of the helpless members of the tribe of more importance than an assault on the soldiers at that moment.

But, so chagrined was Custer at his failure to snare the head chiefs desired, he had completely overlooked the ordinary precaution of posting sentinels within sight of the enemy's camp. Consequently it was not until next morning that he discovered his next door neighbors had extended their safety zone by several miles.

Soon after disarming and securing his four hostages, Custer told them to choose one of their number to bear a message to Medicine Arrow. A selection was made almost immediately. The messenger was instructed to tell Medicine Arrow that the hostages would not be surrendered until the white prisoners were given up and the Cheyennes had agreed to move onto their reservation at Camp Supply. He also was instructed to tell Little Robe that Custer would guarantee him safe return to his people if he should come to headquarters and talk things over.

Night came, but no word from Medicine Arrow. There was a call from the darkness. Custer appealed to Monahseetah for an explanation. She said it was from young braves who had come to see what had been done with Custer's hostages. Through Monahseetah, Custer invited them to come and see for themselves. Fearing a trap, they refused. Taking

Monahseetah with him, Custer went out past the
pickets to meet them. Then he beat a hasty retreat
when he discovered there were four Indians in the
group. Monahseetah finally prevailed upon her
friends to come down to the picket line and talk to
Custer. From there they went with Custer and his
girl friend to visit the hostages held under heavy
guard. As they departed, Custer sent another message by them to Medicine Arrow, saying he would release his captives upon return by the Indians of the
two white women they held.

Throughout the remainder of the night and next
morning Custer waited in vain for a reply to his demands. That afternoon Little Robe appeared. But
Little Robe's visit was far from comforting. He said
the Cheyennes had mistrusted Custer from the first.
Custer's action in seizing hostages immediately after
smoking the peace pipe and assuring those with
whom he had smoked in the Arrow Lodge that his was
a peaceful mission had convinced even the most
trusting that his word could not be relied upon; that
he would do them harm if he had the opportunity.

Little Robe also informed Custer that those in authority in the larger village were unalterably opposed to surrendering the rights granted them by
the Medicine Lodge pact. These included the right
to roam their reservation at will, so long as they,
themselves, lived up to their treaty obligations.
This the Cheyennes insisted they had done. They
felt that the Government had violated its promises
by sending soldiers into their midst, killing many of
their people, and by withholding the issues guaran-
teed in the treaty. Little Robe also expressed doubt
that they would yield their captives or go to Camp
Supply until the Government did make good its part
of the contract.

As he departed, however, Little Robe promised
to do what he could to mediate the present situation.

Another night passed, even more uneventful than the first. Finally one of Little Robe's subordinates reported to Custer. He said the Indians felt Custer personally had broken faith with them by seizing hostages; that until these prisoners were returned as evidence that the white chief acknowledged his error and was willing to keep faith in the future, they would not even discuss surrender of their women captives, nor would they consider placing their people under control and in jeopardy of the soldiers. Custer's actions since coming to the Sweetwater left them no alternative but to fear he might kill them all, just as he tried to do with their friends on the Washita.

The situation was anything but satisfactory to Custer. Instead of intimidating the Indians as he had expected, seizure of the hostages merely had angered them and had made them afraid to trust their families to the questionable mercy of the soldiers. Already he had abandoned hope of being able to induce them to go to Camp Supply without force; yet he was hardly prepared to risk this extremity. Like those of the red men, mounts of the soldiers were weak from lack of provender. They were in no condition to engage in a struggle such as was bound to occur, should force be attempted. Then, too, the soldiers had been reduced to half rations. This meant they did not dare remain much longer away from their main store of supplies which had been left near the western extremities of the Wichitas, instead of being carried on the long trip to the Staked Plains. Much as he disliked to admit it, Custer was forced to the conclusion that the best he could hope for was release of the women prisoners.

This, then, became the burden of further negotiations. He sent word that, unless the women were delivered immediately, he would move his troops to the proximity of the Indian camp again.

Again the Indians refused to yield.

Custer became desperate. He transferred his entire command to a point only two miles distant from the Indian village. There he invited the chiefs of the village into conference with him again. They displayed their confidence in being able to take care of themselves by accommodating him. There they received Custer's ultimatum: that, unless the women were surrendered to him by sundown of the following day, the hostages would be hanged.

Apparently believing from this proposal that Custer had receded from his demand that the village go to Camp Supply and, believing that the hostages would be exchanged for the women, Medicine Arrow sent forward his captives well within the specified time. They were delivered to a delegation selected by Custer from the Kansas volunteers, the transfer being made some distance from the soldier lines. Patiently the Indians waited for the soldiers to bring back the hostages held by Custer. When several minutes had passed and their friends had not been returned to them, the leaders of the Indian contingent sent a messenger to the soldier camp to inquire the cause of this delay.

Custer told them the hostages would not be yielded there; that the Indians would have to come to Camp Supply to get them; that they would have to surrender the entire village there.

Once more there were ominous rumblings in the Indian village. Once more there was insistent demand by warriors that their chiefs lead them in an attack on the soldiers while the village should be scattering beyond reach of their enemies.

Once more the blustering, bluffing Custer lost his nerve, just as he had done a few months previously, when he beat a hasty retreat from Black Kettle's smoldering village, forsaking the missing Elliott detachment to whatever its fate might be. He decided to get out of the enemy's country as quickly as possible.

Custer had gone after this Cheyenne village to bring it into the reservation. His command outnumbered the Indian warriors several to one. Yet, now, actually in contact with them and realizing the impossibility of attempting to carry out these plans, discretion routed his vainglorious, original resolve. He was glad to seize upon the rescue of two white prisoners as a substitute objective of the expedition and to recede from his first—annihilation or capitulation of the entire Cheyenne band.

That night Custer issued orders for his command to march for Camp Supply at daybreak.

At daybreak the column was on its way.

Behind him Custer left those he had set out to bring in. He carried with him two white women obtained from their captors by treachery; also three decrepit old Indian hostages he held in violation of his sacred promise.

Two of these three hostages were destined never to see their people again. While held prisoners in a stockade at Fort Hays, one was shot to death, another was bayoneted to death, the third was clubbed to the ground, unconscious.¹

1. The killing of Big Head and Dull Knife and the brutal beating of Fat Bear at Fort Hays was just one of several tragic aftermaths of the Washita campaign.

At Fort Hays these three warriors were imprisoned in a stockade along with the women and children Custer had captured on the Washita. For awhile, they were permitted to live in tents with the others. Then it was decided to remove the three men to the blockhouse adjoining the camp.

An armed guard of soldiers entered the stockade to remove them. No interpreter was there to explain the move. Believing the braves were being taken away to be executed, women as well as the men attacked the soldiers with knives. The sergeant in command was stabbed in the back by one of the squaws. The soldiers opened fire. Big Head fell, dead. Dull Knife was pierced through the body by a bayonet and later died from the wound. Fat Bear was clubbed with a musket butt, but was not killed.

Custer was at Fort Hays at the time.

CUSTER BREAKS FAITH

Custer's Washita campaign, conceived in treachery, born in treachery, carried out in treachery, closed in treachery.

As rapidly as weary horses could carry them, as fast as footsore and hungry men could march, Custer returned to Camp Supply. He struck the Washita on his return, near where Sergeant Major Kennedy, Major Elliott and fourteen other members of the Seventh Cavalry had lost their lives. There he found the supply train and the remainder of the Kansas regiment awaiting him. Northward the reunited command made its way, past the Antelope Hills, across the Canadian, down Wolf Creek to his goal. There orders reached him, calling him and his command to Fort Hays.

To Fort Hays he led them. There the Kansas volunteers were mustered out and his Seventh regulars went into camp to await orders. There the three hostages were consigned to the stockade to join the Cheyenne women and children Custer had carried away after the Black Kettle massacre. There Custer took leave of Monahseetah. There he was joined by his wife who had remained at Fort Leavenworth while he was in the field.

From there, at the close of the summer, he went to Fort Leavenworth where he began to pen his memoirs. Better those relating to his conquest of the Southern Plains had remained unpenned. For two generations and part of a third they have given his readers a false impression of the liberty-loving, long-suffering, original Americans whom he conquered by the blood of innocents. These he had called "barbarians," "savages."

But Custer's treacherous acts, finally his violation of the Sacred Arrows, was not to be forgotten by the Cheyennes. Some of this very band he had defrauded on the Sweetwater was in on Custer's finish at the Battle of Little Big Horn.

One of them was Magpie.

CHAPTER TWELVE

Echoes of the Washita

THAT same summer most of the Cheyennes and Arapahoes reported to Camp Supply, soon to be honored by the more pretentious title of "Fort Supply". Though extremely skeptical of the white man's sincerity, at least doubtful of the certainity of his making good his promises, they still were willing to accord him one more opportunity to provide for them in such manner as would relieve them of anxiety regarding the future safety and security of their families.

Those of these tribes who had surrendered at Fort Cobb and Fort Sill were sent to their new destinations. A few bands, most of them small in numbers, remained for a while on the plains of Texas. A few stealthily roamed the Washita, ever watchful for scouting soldiers.

One band of Arapahoes, approximately one hundred lodges, quit that region and rejoined their old neighbors, the Gros Ventures, in the far North. They established themselves on Milk River.

One group of Medicine Arrows' band of Cheyennes also departed for the land of long, deep snows. Included in this contingent were Magpie, Big Man, Yellow Horse, Sand Hill Chief, and their families. To them the call of the wilderness was irresistible. They were not yet ready to give up the nomadic life of their ancestors in exchange for the prosaic existence of a reservation Indian with all its demoralizing influences. Besides, some needed to remain free to avenge the Sacred Arrows, should they ever be able to contact Custer again.

Far to the north, they knew, there were hunting grounds where buffalo still were plentiful. There they would be welcomed by their kinsmen, the Northern Cheyennes, and by the Sioux.

After many vicissitudes, they made their way back to the Black Hills, to Tongue River, to Powder River, to the Rosebud. Magpie was wounded twice by soldier bullets during an encounter with Crook's expedition there, a few days before the Sacred Arrows were destined to be avenged on the Little Big Horn. He participated in the aftermath of Custer's last fight. He carried away from that historic battlefield four carbines, and four revolvers, picked up near the dead bodies of members of that same Seventh Cavalry who had chased him and had wounded him and had killed so many of his people on the Washita.

Not until nearly a decade had passed from the time he saw Custer leaving the Sweetwater, did Magpie and his people return to their old stomping ground in the South. By that time, those whom Custer had carried away from the Washita—women and children—had been returned to their people. By that time, two of those whom Custer had dragged as hostages, from the Sweetwater, had been killed by their guards. By that time all of their former associates had become established on their permanent reservation.

But Camp Supply did not remain their concentration point long. Soon the Government discovered that location was not within the boundaries of their legitimate reservation. Nor did it suit the Indians. There was a scarcity of lasting fresh water in that vicinity. Timber was scant. The lands of their hereditary enemies, the untrustworthy Osages, adjoined on the east. It was too close the borderline of Kansas, encouraging marauding Whites to slip into their midst and tempt young men of the

KICKING BIRD

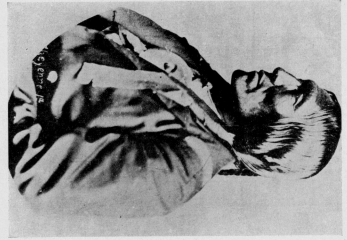

LITTLE ROBE

tribes to molest outlying white settlements by re-taliatory raids.

Their pleas for more suitable surroundings fell upon sympathetic ears when a special commission came from Washington to investigate conditions. When they asked permission to move farther down the North Fork of the Canadian River, where all conditions would be more in keeping with their needs, they found attentive listeners. Their cause was advanced when Medicine Arrow went so far as to agree to go North and induce the Northern Cheyennes and Arapahoes to join them, if they should be granted their request for a satisfactory agency. This was a clinching proposal. The Government was very desirous of uniting Northern Cheyennes and Northern Arapahoes with their tribesmen in the South.

The petitioners were told their request for a new location would be granted. The Government then selected an area near the present site of Pond Creek; but this, too, proved unsatisfactory. The Osages still were too near. The water in that vicinity was not sweet.

Then came Brinton Darlington, their new Quaker agent. He, too, was sympathetic. He, too, wanted his wards satisfied. Not only was this necessary to insure a continuation of peace, but it was considered just. The aged Quaker determined that he would do everything within his power to bring justice to these abused peoples, as soon as possible.

He asked them to suggest a location. They proposed a spot in the valley of the North Fork of the Canadian, near where the Chisholm cattle trail crossed this stream. They said good water was to be found in the sandhills north of there, immense springs that never failed, springs that had been serving cattlemen for years as a camping place while driving their trail herds from the grazing lands of Texas to to the railroad markets of Kansas. There were dwarf oaks on the sandhill ridges while in the numerous bends of the river below was an abundance of large cottonwoods, elms and hackberries.

Agent Darlington proposed that a number of chiefs go with him and representatives of the army to inspect this location. They consented. Everything was found to be as the Indians had described that region. The locations was satisfactory to all concerned, even to Washington.

Without waiting for construction of agency buildings, the Indians began moving almost immediately. Soon their permanent agency was in operation on the new site. Agency buildings were to be erected on the north side of the river, two miles south of Caddo Springs, best known of all the watering places between Texas and Kansas.

Once more California Joe rode into the picture. One day, early in the summer of 1870, he came piloting a strange cavalcade down the trail from Abilene, Kansas, nearest railroad station at that time. Behind this picturesque guide trailed a train of heavy wagons bringing the dismantled sawmill specified in the Medicine Lodge pact. With the train also came artisans, carpenters, blacksmiths. The dismantled sawmill was assembled not far from the agent's headquarters. Within a few days the large circular saw was biting its way through cottonwood, elm, blackjack, postoak and chittam logs cut from the banks of the river nearby.

An agent's house, a commissary, a blacksmith's shop and other essential structures were built from this crude lumber. The Government at last was beginning to keep one of its treaty promises.

Thus came into being the first settlement, Indian agency though it was, in what later was to become Oklahoma Territory. This settlement soon became known as "Darlington" in honor of its founder. Within a short time it grew to be the metropolis of this vast new land of promise. As its importance increased, a stageline was established from Darlington to Vinita, Indian Territory, and from Darlington to Mobeetie, Texas, intersecting at Darlington the older stageline from Kansas to Texas.

But it was nearly two and one-half years after signing of the Medicine Lodge treaty, which had promised the Cheyennes and Arapahoes such a capital, before the Great White Father really began making good most of his pledges. And the Indians could not understand such procrastination. Nor could they discover justice in a situation where the Indian had to deliver at once under penalty of extermination whereas the white man could take his own sweet time about it.

Even then the white man seemed loath to carry out all provisions of his contract with his red brother. Unrest grew until a delegation of chiefs went to Washington to talk to the Great White Father in person and see if they could not expedite matters.[1]

Similar were conditions nearly one hundred miles south where the Kiowas and Comanches, and their few Apache neighbors, were wavering near the threshold which was to lead them from so-called barbarism into civilization. And, as Satanta so eloquently explained to the special commissioners, they were "trying to walk the white man's road," but so far had found nothing along it for them except "hard corn which hurt their teeth; no coffee, no sugar."

There, too, in the immediate vicinity of the Kiowa-Comanche-Apache agency, water was scarce. Timber for fuel had to be brought from the moun-

1. See Appendix M for speeches made by Little Raven and Stone Calf on this occasion.

tains. There was not a sufficiency of grazing for the animals of the troops and those of all the Indians. There, too, the proximity of soldiers and Indians was nettlesome, both to the red men and to the troops.

From there, too, went a delegation of chiefs to Washington to talk over things with the Great White Father.

But the Kiowas and Comanches did not have an agent as sympathetic and as resourceful as Brinton Darlington. Their contacts with troublemaking Whites of Texas and the meddlesome Mexicans were a further source of annoyance which eventually brought on raids and clashes. It was during these trying days that Satanta, Satank and Big Tree became involved in an attack on a wagon train, which led to their arrest at Fort Sill, to Satank's killing and to trial and conviction by the civil courts of Texas for Satanta and Big Tree.

Nor was the situation to be quieted until new outbreaks of a general nature resulted. While the Kiowas and Comanches were being aggravated beyond endurance in the region west of the Washita, intruders from the North were stirring up hostilities along the North Fork of the Canadian. They brought whisky into the lands of the Cheyennes and Arapahoes. They stole the Indians' horses to sell them on Kansas markets. They invaded the Indians' hunting grounds and started slaughtering buffalo for the hide market. The Government was short in its issues. Hunger and pestilence added to miseries of the Indians.

White horse thieves came down from Kansas and ran off a herd of animals belonging to Little Raven. Little Raven's son and a party trailed them as far as the Kansas line. There the Indians were fired upon by soldiers along the border. The son of Little Raven was wounded.

Unable to obtain redress from the Government, the red men took matters into their own hands. The Comanches organized a warpath to drive white hide hunters away from their buffalo herds. They were joined by a few Kiowas, a few Lipans and by some Cheyennes. They attacked the hide hunters in their rendezvous known as Adobe Walls.

For these breaches of the peace, all except a few bands were branded hostiles by the Government. Blood soaked the Plans in more than one spot before the situation could be calmed again.

Custer was heading for his last roundup of red men in Montana when peace finally settled down over the Southern Plains.

＊　　᠍ ᠊　　＊　　　＊

On the banks of the North Fork of the Canadian River, five miles by the winding stream above El Reno, Oklahoma, stands a straggling group of dilapidated old buildings. Yawning excavations here and there disclose the fact that other structures, some of them far more pretentious than those still standing, once kept them company. Where drifting sands and accumulating debris have not completely hidden the walls of these relics, disintegrating stones attest their ancient origin.

New pine boards, conspicuous against a drab background of weather-stained surfaces, indicate an heroic effort has been made to maintain a few of the better buildings in a habitable state. But, for the most part, sagging roofs, crumbling chimneys, gapping apertures in which once were framed multipaned windows of long ago, tottering verandas, shattered weatherboarding and sinking foundations condemn them to oblivion at no distant date, after more than half a century of faultless, faithful service.

Distinctly alien to its natural surroundings, a grove of maples in their prime stands apart from ragged cottonwoods and spreading elms, failing remnants of Western Oklahoma's first tree-planting efforts. Another cluster, this of middle-aged elms and hackberries, reveals a later gesture toward effacing the scars left by Western Oklahoma's first sawmill. Yet, gaunt, lifeless arms among live branches and multitudinous ring growths on stumps, stumps left by the wood-reaper's saw, bear mute evidence that most of the hands of those who gave these trees their opportunity for scenic beautification long ago were folded across bosoms that expanded with pride as this pioneering landscaping task was finished.

Outlining the southern boundary of this historic spot, "Old Man River" is doing his part to obliterate traces of this early occupation before appreciative scions of those responsible for its being can reconstruct the intriguing story of the noble part it played in the merciless vanquishment of a race whose only offense in the beginning was insistence that it be permitted to continue, unhampered by an alien, invading host, its enjoyment of life, liberty and the pursuit of happiness.

His shifting channel has destroyed most of the high, wind-built sanddunes which long ago had sheltered modest skincovered lodges of hundreds of once proud warrior-hunters. He has carried away in his flood waters the dust and the bones and the priceless trinkets of Indian dead buried in these selfsame sepulchers of sand. He has caused abandonment of the roadway over which the post water train, with its bluecoated guard plodded its way, year after year, from never-failing springs in the sandhills to Fort Reno. Fort Reno had come into being during the troublesome days of the middle 'seventies. Only a dim path through the thickets which now cover the bottoms marks the course of this once busy thoroughfare.

Such is the spectral remnant of Darlington, first metropolis of the last frontier; Darlington, last contact point of civilization with the last of the wild, nomadic tribes of the prairies; Darlington, melting pot in which was smelted the modern artistries and the Christian learnings of Cheyennes and Arapahoes; Darlington, where the struggling stage lines from seething Caldwell to hustling Henryetta crossed the stageline from vivacious Vinita to bustling Mobeetie; where was located the first singing sawmill in the land of the Plains Indians; where held forth such picturesque characters as Jack Stilwell, hero of the Arickaree, California Joe, Ben Clark, General Sheridan, General Miles, Johnny Murphy, George Bent and John H. Seger, men who played such prominent roles in bringing the red man to the white man's road and teaching him how to travel it in safety.

It was toward Darlington that Patrick Hennessey was leading a wagon train when attacked and slain by recalcitrant Indians from the Cheyenne-Arapaho reservation, an epic of that period. It was from Darlington that irate warriors quit their reservation to defend by force their treaty rights when trespassing buffalo hunters took up headquarters at Adobe Walls and began exterminating last remnants of the southern bison herds. It was at Darlington the soldiers seized Satanta to lead him back to prison and to tragic death.

It was from Darlington that Dull Knife and Little Wolf, Northern Cheyenne chiefs, started their memorable return trek to the Black Hills. This spectacular pilgrimage will live forever in history as the most dramatic incident of the entire conquest of the southern prairies. It was a determined, defiant, sanguinary march in which three score braves, though encumbered by more than two hundred women and children, baffled more than ten thousand soldiers and frontiersmen striving to turn them back.

It was Darlington's importance which caused establishment of Fort Reno. It was Darlington's preeminence in those days which caused Fort Reno to be made the headquarters post of the southwestern frontier over Fort Sill and Fort Arbuckle.

Transfer of the Darlington property to the state as a home for narcotic addicts, after its most valuable land holdings had been detached, formed a transaction which played an important part in the first successful impeachment of an Oklahoma governor.

Today it is a wild life refuge, a state game farm, seeking restoration of some of the game birds once so plentiful in the days when the wild tribes roamed these regions at will.

The Washita still is the land of the Cheyenne, the Arapahoe, the Kiowa and the Comanche. A few Apaches still reside along its watershed. All are endeavoring to travel the white man's road. Those like Little Raven, Stone Calf, Lone Wolf, Medicine Arrow, Little Robe, Satanta and Kicking Bird, who were first to try this strange trail, found it difficult and treacherous. They found it beset by more hazards then the buffalo trails they had followed in the days before Custer came.

Most of these great red knights and their immediate descendants have passed on. Not more than a dozen of those who were encamped along the banks of that crystal, winding, wooded stream in the autumn of 1868 are left to see its now turbid waters slinking slowly past the remnants of Old Fort Cobb, the ruins of Fort Arbuckle and of Fort Wichita, to lose themselves in those of Red River.

Gone are the buffalo, the deer, the elk and the antelope and wild turkey. Only a few pinnated grouse and scattered conveys of bobwhites may be found in that region now.

Gone is all but a trace of that big bend in the Washita, south of the Antelope Hills, where the squaw of Black Kettle pitched her last tepee. White man has straightened the river there. Even the earth has yielded up the remains of two of the Washita's martyrs, those of Black Kettle, himself, and those of Hawk, one of the two Indian youths who deliberately sacrificed their own lives that women and children might be spared. They were turned up by white men building those arteries of commerce which brought all but extermination to the Plains Indians—a railroad and a highway.

Gone, too, at last, is the once popular belief that the Plains Indian was a merciless, swashbuckling savage, devoid of any of the finer sensibilities of which Civilization prides herself.

But the Battle of the Washita still echoes from one end of the Plains to the other; and from the Atlantic to the Pacific, when one tunes his ear to the story of Custer and those he termed "barbarians."

THE END

Appendix

TABLE OF CONTENTS

APPENDIX A

After 1864, Indians always viewed with suspicion the approach to their village of any considerable body of troops. This was because of the treacherous act of soldiers under Colonel John M. Chivington, who attacked and massacred most of the inhabitants of a Cheyenne and Arapahoe village on Sand Creek, Colorado, November 29, 1864.

This village had surrendered to the military at Fort Lyon, in keeping with a promise of amnesty and protection given its chiefs by Governor Evans, Colonel Chivington and E. W. Wynkoop, agent. Black Kettle, head chief of all the Cheyennes, who had arranged this surrender, barely escaped with his life. His wife was wounded many times, but survived. The patriarchal chief, White Antelope, and several other leaders, together with a large number of their followers, variously estimated from 120 to 350, not only were shot down while claiming protection of an American flag and a white flag of truce but their bodies were atrociously mutilated. Most of those killed were women and children.

So uncalled for was this attack and so fiendish the practices of the white soldiers participating, that Congress ordered a special investigation which resulted in universal condemnation of those responsible. Some of the details are unprintable, but herewith are published a few excerpts from the sworn testimony in a government document known as "Condition of Indian Tribes, 1867."

Page 96. ROBERT BENT, interpreter for Major Anthony at Fort Lyon:

> When we came in sight of the camp, I saw the American flag waving and heard Black Kettle tell the Indians to stand around the flag, and there they were huddled — men, women and children. This was when we were within fifty yards of the Indians. I also saw a white flag raised. After the firing (commenced) the

warriors put the squaws and children together and surrounded them to protect them. I saw five squaws under a bank for shelter. When the troops came up to them, they ran out and showed their persons to let the soldiers know they were squaws and begged for mercy, but the soldiers shot them all. I saw one squaw lying on the bank whose leg had been broken by a shell; a soldier came up to her with drawn sabre; she raised her arm to protect herself, when he struck, breaking her arm; she rolled over and raised her other arm, when he struck, breaking it, and then left her without killing her. There seemed to be an indiscriminate slaughtering of men, women and children. There were thirty or forty squaws collected in a hole for protection; they sent out a little girl about six years old with a white flag on a stick; she had not preceded but a few steps when she was shot and killed. All the squaws in that hole were afterward killed, and four or five bucks outside. Everyone I saw dead was scalped. I saw one squaw cut open with an unborn child, as I thought, lying by her side. Captain Soule afterwards told me that such was a fact.

Page 61. JAMES OLNEY, First Colorado Cavalry:

During the massacre I saw three squaws and five children, prisoners in charge of some soldiers that while they were being brought in they were approached by Lieutenant Harry Richmond of the Third Colorado Cavalry; that Lieutenant Richmond thereupon immediately killed and scalped the three women and five children while they (the prisoners) were screaming for mercy; while the soldiers in whose charge these prisoners were shrank back, apparently aghast."

Page 72. ASBURY BIRD, First Colorado Cavalry:

I should judge there were between 400 and 500 Indians killed. I went over the ground soon after the battle. I counted 350 lying up and down the creek.

Page 73. LIEUTENANT CRAMER, First Colorado Cavalry:

The women and children were huddled together and most of our fire was concentrated on them. * * * Our force was so large that there was no necessity of firing on the Indians. We had the assurance of Major Anthony that Black Kettle and his friends should be saved, and only those Indians who had committed depredations should be harmed. * * * I told Colonel Chivington of the position in which the officers stood from Major Wynkoop's pledges to the Indians, and also Major Anthony's, and that it would be murder in every sense of the word, if he attacked those Indians. His reply was, bringing his fist down close to my face, "Damn any man who sympathizes with the Indians.' I told him what pledges were given the Indians." He replied "That he had come to kill Indians, and believed it to be honorable under any and all circumstances," all this at Fort Lyon. Lieutenant Dunn went to Chivington and wanted to know if he could kill his prisoner, young Smith. His reply was 'Don't ask me, you know my orders: I want to prisoners.' (Smith was killed)

Page 75. AMOS C. MIKSCH, Corporal, First Colorado Cavalry:

I was in the battery; did not see the first attack; after we came up we opened fire on the Indians; they retreated and we followed and stayed until all were killed we could find. Next morning, after the battle, I saw a little boy covered up among the Indians in a trench, still alive. I saw a major in the third regiment take out his pistol and blow off the top of his head. I saw some men unjointing fingers to get rings off and cutting off ears to get silver ornaments. I saw a party with the same major take up bodies that had been buried in the night, to scalp them and take off ornaments. Next morning, after they were dead and stiff, these men pulled out the bodies of the squaws and pulled them open in an indecent manner. * * * In the afternoon I saw twenty-five or thirty women and children; Colonel Chivington would not allow them to come in; a squad of the Third Colorado was sent out; I do not know what became of them.

REPORT OF THE BOARD OF INDIAN COMMISSIONERS, 1869, Page 15.

The history of these Indians, since first brought into treaty stipulations with the United States, is one of almost unmitigated wrongs endured. In peace, they have been the frequent victims of murderers and marauders, and the constant prey of traders and agents. In war, their own barbarities, have, on some occasions, been more than emulated by their white enemies. This simple narration of their story would compel, from mere feelings of commiseration, the most generous treatment on the part of the government, and it would seem that no amount of generosity now practicable would be sufficient to make amends for the past. * * * *

In 1851, September 17, a treaty was concluded which, while it did not deprive the Indians of the right of transit and hunting over any other land claimed by them, confirmed their title to * * * * the largest and most valuable part of Colorado, a portion of Dakota and Nebraska and the western part of Kansas, equal in all to about one hundred thousand square miles. In consideration of their abandonment of all title to other lands, except their hunting, fishing and transit rights * * * * the United States bound themselves "to protect the aforesaid Indian nations against the commission of all depredations by the people of the United States after ratification of this treaty." They also further agreed to pay the Arapahoes and Cheyennes the sum of fifty thousand dollars per annum for the term of fifty years.

After the Indians had signed the treaty, the United States reduced the term for which payment was to be made from fifty to ten years. To this change the Indians never gave their assent; nevertheless, with the change, the treaty was proclaimed and assumed to be operative by both parties. No one had ever pretended to aver that the Indians broke the treaty, nor, on the other hand, do we find anything on record to show that the United States ever seriously attempted to comply with their agreement to protect said Indians against the commission of "all depredations by the people of the United States." The wonderful influx of population into Colorado, and the subsequent events, indicates the extent of protection afforded. The white man, in his greed for gain, robbed them of their homes and hunting grounds, and, when they dared to complain, found justification only in the heartless and brutal maxim that "the Indian has no rights which the white man is bound to respect," a sentiment in which the government quietly acquiesced.

In 1861, the United States, having utterly failed to carry into effect the stipulations of the existing treaty, the Indians were induced, on the 18th of February, to make another. * * * It will be seen by the new treaty that the Indians yielded their right to the immense territory before confirmed to them, and accepted a comparatively small district in the southern part of Colorado. In lieu of the lands conceded, the United States agreed to pay the two tribes $60,000 per annum for fifteen years, and to break up and fence lands, build houses for the chiefs, stock the farms with horses, cattle, etc., and supply agricultural implements, erect mills, and maintain engineers, millers, farmers and mechanics among them, and to protect them "in the quiet and peaceable possession" of their reservation.

The savages, it is alleged, maintained inviolate their part of this treaty, also, and in 1864 (after three years had elapsed) the government had commenced some of the permanent improvements promised. In April of that year, an officer of the United States, in command of forty men, attempted to disarm a party of Cheyennes supposed to have stolen horses, and whom he had invited forward to talk with him. This naturally brought on a fight between the parties. The small portion of Colorado still occupied by the Indians was too much for the cupidity of the inhabitants of the Territory. and they seized with avidity upon the pretext of this affair to set about their expulsion or extermination. For the honor of humanity, it would be well could the record of their deeds in this behalf be blotted out. The entire history of Indian warfare furnishes no more black and damning episode than the massacre of Sand Creek.

After the expenditure of $30,000.00 in the persecution of a war, which, in the language of the late peace commission was "dishonorable to the nation and disgraceful to those who originated it," a treaty of peace was concluded at the camp on the Little Arkansas, October 14, 1865.

This treaty deprived them (the Indians) of the remainder of their Colorado possessions * * * *.

The United States also stipulated to expend annually for the benefit of these Indians during forty years, a sum equal to $40.00 per capita, and until removed to their new home, they were "expressly permitted to reside upon and range at pleasure throughout the unsettled portions of the country they claim as originally theirs, between the Arkansas and Platte Rivers." Article IX provided for the payment of all arrears accrued under former treaties. When the treaty went before the senate for ratification, that body altered Article IX to read, "upon the ratification of this treaty, all former treaties are hereby abrogated," and added further a provision that "no part of the (new) reservation shall be within the State of Kansas or upon any reserve belonging to any other Indian tribe or tribes, without their consent."

The largest and best part of the reservation was "within the limits of Kansas" and the remainder within the reserve long before granted, and belonging to, the Cherokees. Thus, by the process of two treaties, between the civilized and the savage, the strong and the weak, the Arapahoes and Cheyennes were stripped of their magnificent possessions, larger than the States of Pennsylvania, New York and New Jersey, and left without a foot of land they could call their home. They had still left to them the hunting and "roaming" privileges between the Arkansas and Platte Rivers. The sequel shows that even that was considered too much for them.

The breaking out of the Sioux War of 1866 in Minnesota was made the occasion for suspicion that the Cheyennes and Arapahoes intended war also, and that suspicion was made the opportunity for driving them from their hunting grounds, where their presence was supposed to be "calculated to bring about collision with the whites."

On the 28th of October, 1867, the treaty of Medicine Lodge Creek was concluded by the peace commission, and now is in force. It designated the reservation by the following boundaries * * *. The country within these limits contains but little arable land, is almost destitute of timber, and has very little permanent fresh water. * * * On the east it is joined by the Osages, the heriditary enemies of the Cheyennes, and the location for the agency is so near Kansas on the north as to render too easy the predatory excursions of both Indians and white men over their respective borders.

The Indians also urge these objections to the reservation and claim that they supposed, when they signed the treaty, that their country extended to the main Canadian and consequently included the North Fork. * * * * Little Raven and Medicine Arrow, the chiefs, both assert that they never, until it was made known to them during the present summer, understood rightly the real bounds of their reservation. * * * *

While the history of the Cheyenne treaties must convince everyone interested in the subject that the United States, by its own acts, owe to these Indians at least the degree of justice we have recommended, it also forcibly illustrates the injudiciousness and iniquity of the treaty system as heretofore practiced. In its notable features it does not differ materially from the history of other treaties.

The United States first creates the fiction that a few thousand savages stand in the position of equality to capacity, power and right of negotiation with a great civilized nation. They next proceed to impress upon the savages, with all the forms of treaty and solemnity of parchment, signatures, and seals, the preposterous idea that they are the owners in fee of the fabulous tracts of country over which their nomadic habits have permitted them or their ancestors to roam. The title being thus settled, they purchase and promise payment for a portion of territory and further bind themselves in the most solemn manner to protect and defend the Indians in the possession of some immense remainder defined by boundaries in the treaty, thus becoming, as it were, particeps criminis with the savages in resisting the "encroachments" of civilization and the progressive movement of the age. Having entered into this last-named, impracticable obligation, the fact of its non-performance becomes the occasion of disgraceful and expensive war to subdue their victims to the point of submission to another treaty. And so the tragedy of war and the farce of treaty have been enacted again and again, each time with increasing shame to the nation.

APPENDIX C

MEDICINE LODGE TREATY
(Cheyenne-Arapahoe)

Treaty between the United States of America and the Cheyenne and Arapahoe Tribes of Indians, Concluded October 28, 1867; ratification advised July 25, 1868; proclaimed August 19, 1868.

ANDREW JOHNSON, President of the United States of America, to all singular to whom these presents shall come, greeting:

Whereas, a treaty was made and concluded at the Council Camp, on Medicine Lodge Creek, seventy miles south of Fort Larned, in the State of Kansas, on the twenty-eighth day of October, in the year of our Lord, one thousand eight hundred and sixty-seven, by and between N. G. Taylor, Brevet Major-General William S. Harney, Brevet Major-General C. C. Augur, Brevet Major-General Alfred H. Terry, John B. Sanburn, Samuel F. Tappan, and J. B. Henderson, commissioners on the part of the United States, and O-to-ah-nac-co (Bull-Bear) Moke-tav-a-to (Black Kettle), Little Raven, Yellow Bear, and other chiefs and headmen of the Cheyenne and Arapahoe tribes of Indians, on the part of said Indians, and duly authorized thereto by them, which treaty is in the words and figures following, to-wit: Articles of a treaty and agreement made and entered into at the Council Camp on Medicine Lodge Creek, seventy miles south of Fort Larned, in the State of Kansas, on the twenty-eighth day of October, eighteen hundred and sixty-seven, by and between the United States of America, represented by its commissioners duly appointed thereto, to-wit: Nathaniel G. Taylor, William S. Harney, C. C. Augur, Alfred H. Terry, John B. Sanborn, Samuel F. Tappan and John B. Henderson, of the one part and the Cheyenne and Arapahoe tribes of Indians, represented by their chiefs and headmen, duly authorized and empowered to act for the body of the people of said tribes—the names of said chiefs and headmen being hereto subscribed—of the other part, Witness:

ARTICLE I. From this day forward, all war between the parties of this agreement shall forever cease. The Government of the United States desires peace, and its honor is here pledged to keep it. The Indians desire peace, and they now pledge their honor to maintain it.

If bad men among the whites, or among other people subject to the authority of the United States, shall commit any wrong upon the person or property of the Indians, the United States will, upon proof made to the agent and forwarded to the Commissioner of Indian Affairs at Washington, proceed at once to cause the offender to be arrested and punished according to the laws of the United States, and also reimburse the injured person for the loss sustained.

If bad men among the Indians shall commit a wrong or depredation upon the person or property of anyone, white, black, or Indian, subject to the authority of the United States and at peace therewith, the tribes herein named solemnly agree that they will, on proof made to their agent, and notice by him, deliver up the wrong-doer to the United States, to be tried and punished according to its laws; and in case they wilfully refuse so to do, the person injured shall be reimbursed for his loss from the annuities or other moneys due or to become due to them under this or other treaties made with the United States. And the President, on advising with the Commissioner of Indian Affairs, shall prescribe such rules and regulations for ascertaining damages, under the provisions of this article, as in his judgment may be proper. But no damages shall be adjusted and paid until thoroughly examined and passed upon by the Commissioner of Indian Affairs and the Secretary of the Interior, and no one sustaining loss, while violating, or because of his violating the provisions of this treaty of the laws of the United States, shall be reimbursed therefor.

ARTICLE 2. The United States agrees that the following district of country, to-wit: commencing at the point where the Arkansas River crosses the 37th parallel of north latitude, thence west on said parallel—the said line being the southern boundary of the State of Kansas—to the Cimarone River, (sometimes called the Red Fork of the Arkansas River;) thence down said Cimarone River; thence up the Arkansas River, in the middle of the main channel thereof, to the place of beginning, shall be and the same is hereby set apart for the absolute and undisturbed use and occupation of the Indians herein named, and for such other friendly tribes or individual Indians, as from time to time they may be willing, with the consent of the United States, to admit among them; and the United States now solemnly agrees that no persons except those herein authorized so to do, and except such officers, agents, and employes of the Government as may be authorized to enter upon Indian reservations in discharge of duties enjoined by law, shall ever be permitted to pass over, settle upon, or reside in the territory described in this article, or in such territory as may be added to this reservation for the use of said Indians.

ARTICLE 3. If it should appear from actual survey, or other examination of said tract of land, that it contains less than one hundred and sixty acres of tillable land for each person who at the time may be authorized to reside on it, under the provisions of this treaty, and a very considerable number of such persons shall be disposed to commence cultivating the soil as farmers, the United States agrees to set apart for the use of said Indians, as herein provided, such additional quantity of arable land adjoining to said reservation, or as near the same as it can be obtained, as may be required to provide the necessary amount.

ARTICLE 4. The United States agrees at its own proper expenses to construct at some place near the center of said reservation, where timber and water may be convenient, the following buildings, to-wit: a warehouse or store-room for the use of the agent in storing goods belonging to the Indians, to cost not exceeding fifteen hundred dollars; an agency building for the residence of the agent, to cost not exceeding three thousand dollars; a residence for the physician, to cost not more than three thousand dollars; and five other buildings, for a carpenter, farmer, blacksmith, miller, and engineer, each to cost not exceeding two thousand dollars; also a schoolhouse or mission-building, so soon as a sufficient number of children can be induced by the agent to attend school, which shall not cost exceeding five thousand dollars. The United States agrees, further, to cause to be erected on said reservation, near the other buildings herein authorized, a good steam circular saw-mill, with a grist-mill and shingle machine attached, the same to cost not exceeding eight thousand dollars.

ARTICLE 5. The United States agrees that the agent for said Indians in the future shall make his home at the agency building; that he shall reside among them, and keep an office open at all times for the purpose of prompt and diligent inquiry into such matters of complaint by and against the Indians as may be presented for investigation, under the provisions of their treaty stipulations, as also for the faithful discharge of other duties injoined on him by law. In all cases of depredation on person or property, he shall cause the evidence to be taken in writing and forwarded, together with his finding, to the Commissioner of Indian Affairs, whose decision, subject to the revision of the Secretary of the Interior, shall be binding on the parties of this treaty.

ARTICLE 6. If any individual, belonging to said tribes of Indians, or legally incorporated with them, being the head of a family, shall desire to commence farming, he shall have the privilege to select, in the presence and with the assistance of the agent then in charge, a tract of land within said reservation, not exceeding three hundred and twenty acres in extent, which tract, when so selected, certified, and recorded in the land-book as herein directed, shall cease to be held in common, but the same may be occupied and held in the exclusive possession of the person selecting it, and of his family, so long as he or they may continue to cultivate it. Any person over eighteen years of age, not being the head of a family, may in like manner select and cause to be certified to him, or her, for the purpose of cultivation, a quantity of land not exceeding eighty acres in extent, and thereupon be entitled to the exclusive possession of the same as above directed.

For each tract of land so selected, a certificate containing a description thereof, and the name of the person selecting it, with a certificate indorsed thereon, that the same has been recorded, shall be delivered to the party entitled to it by the agent, after the same shall have been recorded by him in a book to be kept in his office, subject to inspection, which said book shall be known as the "Cheyenne and Arapahoe Land Book." The President may at any time order a survey of the reservation and when so surveyed, Congress shall provide for protecting the rights of settlers in their improvements, and may fix the character of the title held by each.

The United States may pass such laws on the subject of alienation and descent of property, and on all subjects connected with the government of the Indians on said reservations, and the internal police thereof as may be thought proper.

ARTICLE 7. In order to insure the civilization of the tribes entering into this treaty, the necessity of education is admitted, especially by such of them are, or may be, settled on said agricultural reservation, and they therefore pledge themselves to compel their children, male and female, between the ages of six and sixteen years, to attend school; and it is hereby made the duty of the agent for said Indians to see that this stipulation is strictly complied with; and the United States agrees that for every thirty children between said ages, who can be induced or compelled to attend school, a house shall be provided, and a teacher, competent to teach the elementary branches of an English education, shall be furnished, who will reside among said Indians, and faithfully discharge his or her duties as a teacher. The provisions of this article to continue for not less than twenty years.

ARTICLE 8. When the head of a family or lodge shall have selected lands and received his certificate as above directed, and the agent shall be satisfied that he intends in good faith to commence cultivating the soil for a living, he shall be entitled to receive seeds and agricultural implements for the first year, not exceeding the value of One Hundred Dollars; and for each succeeding year he shall continue to farm for a period of three years more, he shall be entitled to receive seeds and implements as aforesaid, not exceeding in value twenty-five dollars.

And it is further stipulated that such persons as commence farming shall receive instruction from the farmer herein provided for; and whenever more than one hundred persons shall enter upon the cultivation of the soil, a second blacksmith shall be provided, with such iron, steel, and other material as may be needed.

ARTICLE 9. At any time after ten years from the making of this treaty, the United States shall have the privilege of withdrawing the physician, farmer, blacksmith, carpenter, engineer, and miller, herein provided for, but in case of such withdrawal, an additional sum, thereafter, of ten thousand dollars per annum shall be devoted to the education of said Indians, and the Commissioner of Indian Affairs shall, upon careful inquiry into their condition, make such rules and regulations for the expenditure of said sums as will best promote the educational and moral improvement of said tribes.

ARTICLE 10. In lieu of all sums of money or other annuities provided to be paid to the Indians herein named, under the treaty of October fourteenth, eighteen hundred and sixty-five, made at the mouth of Little Arkansas, and under all treaties made previous thereto, the United States agrees to deliver at the agency house on the reservation herein named, on the fifteenth day of October, of each year, for thirty years, the following articles, to-wit:

For each male person over fourteen years of age, a suit of good, substantial woolen clothing, consisting of coat, pantaloons, flannel shirt, hat, and a pair of home-made socks.

For each female over twelve years of age, a flannel skirt, or the goods necessary to make it, a pair of woolen hose, twelve yards of calico, and twelve yards of cotton domestics.

For the boys and girls under the ages named, such flannel and cotton goods as may be needed to make each a suit as aforesaid, together with a pair of woolen hose for each.

And in order that the Commissioner of Indian

Affairs may be able to estimate properly for the articles herein named, it shall be the duty of the agent each year to forward to him a full and exact census of the Indians on which the estimate from year to year can be based.

And, in addition to the clothing herein named, the sum of Twenty Thousand Dollars shall be annually appropriated for a period of thirty years, to be used by the Secretary of the Interior in the purchase of such articles as, from time to time, the condition and necessities of the Indians may indicate to be proper. And, if, at any time within the thirty years, it shall appear that the amount of money for clothing, under this article, can be appropriated to better uses for the tribe herein named, Congress may, by law, change the appropriation to other purposes; but in no event, shall the amount of this appropriation be withdrawn or discontinued for the period named. And the President shall, annually, detail an officer of the Army to be present, and attest the delivery of all the goods herein named to the Indians, and he shall inspect and report on the quantity and quality of the goods and the manner of their delivery.

ARTICLE 11. In consideration of the advantages and benefits conferred by this treaty, and the many pledges of friendship by the United States, the tribes who are parties to this agreement hereby stipulate that they will relinquish all right to occupy permanently the territory outside of their reservation as herein defined, but they yet reserve the right to hunt on any lands south of the Arkansas, so long as the buffalo may range thereon in such numbers as to justify the chase; and no white settlements shall be permitted on any part of the lands contained in the old reservation as defined by the treaty made between the United States and the Cheyenne, Arapahoe, and Apache tribes of Indians, at the mouth of the Little Arkansas, under date of October fourteenth, eighteen hundred sixty-five, within three years from this date; and they, the said tribes, further expressly agree:

1st. That they will withdraw all opposition to the construction of the railroad now being built on the Smoky Hill River, whether it be built to Colorado or New Mexico.

2nd. That they will permit the peaceable construction of any railroad not passing over their reservation, as herein defined.

3rd. That they will not attack any persons at home or traveling, nor molest or disturb any wagon-trains, coaches, mules, or cattle belonging to the people of the United States, or to persons friendly therewith.

4th. They will never capture or carry off from the settlements white women or children.

5th. They will never kill or scalp white men, nor attempt to do them harm.

6th. They withdraw all pretense of opposition to the construction of the railroad now being built along the Platte River, and westward to the Pacific Ocean; and they will not in the future object to the construction of railroads, wagon-roads, mail-stations, or other works of utility or necessity, which may be ordered or permitted by the laws of the United States. But, should such roads or other works be constructed on the lands of their reservation, the Government will pay the tribe whatever amount of damage may be assessed by three disinterested commissioners to be appointed by the President for that purpose, one of said commissioners to be a chief or head-man of the tribe.

7th. They agree to withdraw all opposition to the military post or roads now established, or that may be established, not in violation of treaties heretofore made or hereafter to be made with any of the Indian tribes.

ARTICLE 12. No treaty for the cession of any portion or part of the reservation herein described, which may be held in common, shall be of any validity or force as against the said Indians, unless executed and signed by at least three-fourths of all the adult male Indians occupying or interested in the same; and no cession by the tribe shall be understood or construed in such manner as to deprive without his consent any individual member of the tribe of his rights to any tract of land selected by him as provided in Article 6 of this treaty.

ARTICLE 13. The United States hereby agree to furnish annually to the Indians the physician. teachers, carpenter, miller, engineer, farmer, and blacksmiths, as herein contemplated, and that

APPENDIX

such appropriations shall be made from time to time on the estimates of the Secretary of the Interior, as will be sufficient to employ such persons.

ARTICLE 14. It is agreed that the sum of five hundred dollars, annually, for three years from date, shall be expended in presents to the ten persons of said tribe who, in the judgment of the agent, may grow the most valuable crops for the respective year.

ARTICLE 15. The tribes herein named agree that when the agency-house and other buildings shall be constructed on the reservation named, they will regard and make said reservation their permanent home, and they will make no permanent settlement elsewhere, but they shall have the right, subject to the conditions and modifications of this treaty, to hunt on the lands south of the Arkansas River, formerly called theirs, in the same manner as agreed on by the treaty of the "Little Arkansas," concluded the fourteenth day of October, eighteen hundred sixty-five.

N. G. TAYLOR, (SEAL)
President of Indian Commission
WM. S. HARNEY, (SEAL)
Major-General, Brevet,
C. C. AUGUR, (SEAL)
Brevet Major-General
ALFRED H. TERRY, (SEAL)
Brevet Major-General
JOHN B. SANBORN, (SEAL)
Commissioner
SAMUEL F. TAPPAN, (SEAL)
J. B. HENDERSON, (SEAL)

ATTEST:—
Ashton S. H. White, Secretary.
Geo. B. Willis, Phonographer

On the part of the Cheyennes:
O-to-ah-nac-co, Bull Bear, his X mark (SEAL)
Moke-tav-a-to, Black Kettle, his X mark (SEAL)
Nac - co - hah-ket, Little Bear, his X mark (SEAL)

On the part of the Arapahoes:
Little Raven, hix X mark (SEAL)
Vip-po-nah, Slim Face, his X mark (SEAL)
Wo-pah-ah, Grey Head, his X mark (SEAL)
O-ni-hah-ket, Little Rock, his X mark (SEAL)

Mo-a-vo-oa-ast, Spotted Elk, his X mark (SEAL)
Is-se-von-ne-ve, Buffalo Chief, his X mark (SEAL)
Wo - po - ham, or White Horse, his X mark (SEAL)
Hah-ket-home-mah, Little Robe, his X mark (SEAL)
Min-min-ne-wah, Whirlwind, his X mark (SEAL)
Mo-uan-histe-histow, Heap of Birds, his X mark (SEAL)

Ma-mo-ki, or Curley Hair, his X mark (SEAL)
O-to-ah-has-tis, Tall Bull, his X mark (SEAL)
Yellow Bear, his X mark (SEAL)
Storm, his X mark (SEAL)
White Rabbit, his X mark (SEAL)
Spotted Wolf, his X mark (SEAL)
Little Big Mouth, his X mark (SEAL)
Young Colt, his X mark (SEAL)
Tall Bear, his X mark (SEAL)

ATTEST: —

C. W. Whitaker, Interpreter
H. Douglas, Major, Third Infantry
Jno. D. Howland, Clerk Indian Commission
Sam'l. S. Smoot, United States Surveyor
A. A. Taylor
Henry Stanley, Correspondent
John S. Smith, United States Interpreter
George Bent, Interpreter
Thos. Murphy, Sup't. Indian Affairs

A similar treaty, almost identical in verbiage, save for the section defining their reservation, was executed with the Kiowas and Comanches. Their reservation was defined:

"Commencing at a point where the Washita River crosses the ninety-eighth meridian, west from Grenwich, thence up the Washita River, in the middle of the main channel thereof to a point thirty miles, by river, west of Fort Cobb as now established; thence due west to the North Fork of the Red River, provided said line strikes said river east of the one hundreth meridian of west longtitude; if not, then only to said meridian line to said North Fork of Red River; thence down said North Fork in the middle of the main channel thereof from the point where it may be first intersected by the lines above described, to the main Red River; thence down said river in the middle of the main channel thereof to its intersection with the ninety-eighth meridian of longtitude, west of Grenwich; thence north of said meridian line to the place of beginning.

N. G. TAYLOR, President of
Indian Commission.
W. S. HARNEY, Brevet Major
General
C. C. AUGUR, Brevet Major
General
ALFRED H. TERRY, Brigadier
and Major General
J. B. SANBORN
SAMUEL F. TAPPAN
J. B. HENDERSON

ATTEST: —

Ashton S. White, Secretary

On the part of the Kiowas: —

Satank, or Sitting Bear
Satanta, or White Bear
Watchkonk, or B l a c k Eagle
Tonoenko, or Kicking Eagle
Fishemore, or Stinking Saddle Cloth

Mayetin, or Woman's Heart
Satimgear, or Stumbling Bear
Sitpargo, or One Bear
Corbean, or the Crow
Satamore, or Bear Lying Down

On the part of the Comanches: —

Parrywahsaymen, or Ten Bears
Teppenavon, or Painted Lips
Tosain, or Silver Brooch
Cearchineka, or Standing Feather
Howear, or Gap in the Woods

Tirhayohnahip or Horse Back
Esananaca, or Wolf's Name
Ahteesta, or Little Horn
Poohyahtoyehbe, or Iron Mountain
Saddyyo, or Dog Fat

ATTEST:

James A. Hardy, Inspector General United States Army
Samuel S. Smoot, United States Surveyor
Philip McCusker, Interpreter
J. H. Leavenworth, United States Indian Agent
Thomas Murphy, Superintendent Indian Affairs
Henry M. Stanley, Correspondent
A. A. Taylor, Assistant Secretary
William Fayel, Correspondent

CONQUEST OF THE SOUTHERN PLAINS

James O. Taylor, Artist
George B. Willis, Phonographer
C. W. Whitaker, Trader

APPENDIX D

REPORT COMMISSIONER OF INDIAN AFFAIRS, 1868, Page 81

PHILADELPHIA, PENNSYLVANIA
October 7, 1868

Sir:

In accordance with your instructions, I would respectfully submit the following report as to the causes, which, in my opinion, have led to the present Indian war now existing with the Indians of my agency, viz., the Cheyennes and Arapahoes.

The war, undoubtedly, would have been prevented had the Government continued to keep up the supply of subsistence that has been furnished them during the spring and early summer. They had gradually got weaned from their old habits to that degree that they depended upon the provisions that were issued to them to sustain them, and consequently it was not necessary for them to scatter out in little bands all over the country, for the purpose of finding game, therefore running a risk of coming into contact with white men, and also being subjected to temptation when hungry; but even after their supplies were stopped, had I been allowed to issue the arms and ammunition to them at the time promised, they still would have been content from the fact of them having the means to procure game; but the failure of the government to fulfill its promises in the latter respect naturally incensed some of the wilder spirits among them, and, consequently, the outrages committed upon the Saline river.

Immediately, upon hearing of said outrages, I was anxious to have the guilty punished, and by that means save those of the different tribes who did not deserve punishment. I saw two of the principal chiefs of the Cheyennes, viz., Medicine Arrow and Little Rock and demanded that they deliver up the perpretators of the aforementioned outrages, which they promised, positively, should be done, but before sufficient time had elapsed for them to fulfill their promises, the troops were in the field, and the Indians in flight.

Even after the majority of the Cheyennes had been forced to take to the warpath in consequence of the bad acts of some of their nation, several bands of the Cheyennes and the whole Arapahoe tribe could have been kept at peace, had proper action been taken at the time, but now all of the Indians of the Upper Arkansas are engaged in the struggle.

Undoubtedly this war could have been prevented, had Congress made an appropriation for the purpose of continuing the supply of subsistence to these Indians, thus following the dictates of Humanity and justice. The expenditure of a few thousands would have saved millions to the country; would have saved hundreds of white men's lives; have saved the necessity of hunting down and destroying innocent Indians for the faults of the guilty; of driving into misery and starvation numbers of women and little children, not one of whom but now mourns some relative brutally murdered by white men at the horrible massacre of Sand Creek, and who still suffer from the loss of their habitations and property, wantonly destroyed by Major General Hancock.

Had each member of Congress seen what I have of the injustices practiced toward these Indians, they would imagine that there was not sufficient money in the United States Treasury to appropriate for their benefit.

With much respect,
Your obedient servant,
E. W. WYNKOOP,
United States Indian
Agent

Hon. Charles E. Mix,
Acting Commissioner Indian Affairs

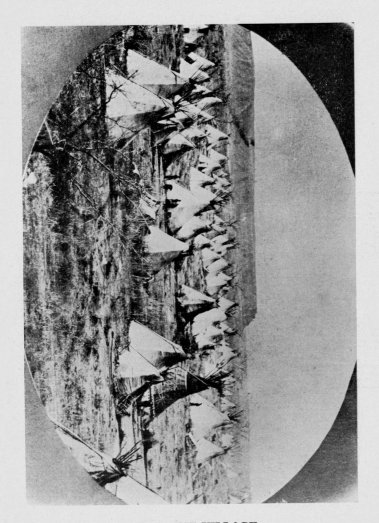

CHEYENNE VILLAGE

From an old photograph made in what is now
Western Oklahoma shortly after the
Washita Campaign

APPENDIX E

REPORT COMMISSIONER OF INDIAN AFFAIRS, 1868, Page 64

COUNCIL GROVE, KANSAS, JUNE 4, 1868

Sir: Under your instructions of the 30th of May, Major Stover and myself started on the 1st of June, arriving at the Kaw Agency in the morning of the 3rd, about 10 o'clock, and found the Kaws much excited; they informed us the Cheyennes were very near and in great numbers, going to attack them; we tried hard to restore quiet, but, before we effected anything, about 80 Cheyennes, Arapahoes and Kiowas charged by their camp without firing a gun; the Kaws shot first, about 20 shots, but the distance was too great to do any damage; the Cheyennes formed on a hill in full view, and, while I was trying to get their numbers, a messenger (a white man) came for Major Stover and myself; said chief wished to talk, having heard as they passed Council Grove that I had arrived that morning; we took horses and started. I took some tobacco as presents and they met us friendly. I informed them I had been sent by their Great White Father to make peace between them and the Kaws, and, while arranging for the council, they expressed their willingness, and said for the Major to bring two Kaws without arms, and they would disarm and send two of their number with me, and would see if peace could not be made; and just then the Kaws fired on us and some of the balls passed close to Major Stover and myself; some passed over our heads and some fell short; he wheeled and went to the Kaws, while the Cheyennes and myself changed position. He could not prevent them from again charging us in our fourth position; firing fast and in great numbers. One of the Cheyennes to whom I was speaking, took my horse by the bridle, after seeing two balls strike under him, and led me outside. The firing then began on both sides;

they fought as all Indians, by charging, circling and firing all the while at random; the fight was in open ground and lasted from three to four hours; we stood over them, seeing it all. Several citizens joined us, and, late in the evening, the Cheyenne chief sounded a retreat, the bugler not missing a note, and I am sure Seigel never took his men off the field in better order; they then fired two stone buildings occupied by half-breeds, passed through Council Grove, where they were furnished with sugar and coffee, and, after leaving, robbed three citizen farmers, are said now to be camped on Diamond Creek, some 18 miles west, waiting for the Kaws to come and fight or make peace. They are also killing what beef they want to subsist their soldiers on. They number about 400 to 500, say principally Cheyennes; the balance are Arapahoes and Comanches and some Kiowas. They informed me that they would not injure the whites unless they came with the Kaws to fight them; seemed glad to see me, and said they would make peace; but I have heard since they want seven scalps. The militia are under arms and, after the excitement is over, if they remain, Major Stover and myself will do all we can to effect a peace between them. More anon.

Respectfully, your obedient servant,

A. G. BOONE, Special Agent.

Hon. N. G. Taylor
Commissioner Indian Affairs.

APPENDIX F

REPORT OF COMMISSIONER OF INDIAN AFFAIRS, 1868, PAGE 266

UPPER ARKANSAS AGENCY
FORT LARNED, KANSAS, SEPTEMBER 10, 1868.

Sir:

I have the honor to submit the following as my second annual report:

Soon after my last annual report, a treaty was held with the Indians of my agency at Medicine Lodge Creek, for the reason that some of these Indians had been, to a certain degree, engaged in hostilities against the whites, having been driven to that course by the mistakes and imprudences of General W. S. Hancock; that treaty was made in good faith by the Indians as well as by the honorable gentlemen who composed the commission.

From the date of the treaty, made at Medicine Lodge Creek, the Indians, including the Cheyennes, Arapahoes and Apaches, were in perfect friendly relation with the whites up to last June, when, while making a foray into the Kaw Indian country, in the neighborhood of Council Grove, Kansas, for the purpose of fighting their enemies, the Kaws, there were some slight depredations committed by some of the young men of the Cheyennes, the details of which affair the department is conversant with. At that time the annuity goods, including a large amount of arms and ammunition, were enroute to my agency, when I became the recipient of an order from yourself not to issue the arms and ammunition, in consequence of their conduct with respect to the whites, while making the raid against the Kaws. When the goods arrived, I was obliged to state to the Indians what my instructions were in regard to the arms and ammunition. As I have heretofore stated, they appeared very much disappointed and could not realize that they had deserved such treatment. Subsequently I received permission from the department to issue them their arms and ammunition, which I accordingly did; but, **a short time before the issue was made,** a war party had started north from the Cheyenne village on the warpath against the Pawnees, they, not knowing of the issue, and smarting under their present unfortunate aspect of affairs. The United States troops (Sully's expedition) are now south of the Arkansas River, in hot pursuit of the Cheyennes, the effect of which, I think, will be to plunge other tribes into the difficulty, and finally culminate in a general Indian war.

I have the honor to be, with much respect, your obedient servant.

E. W. WYNKOOP,
United States Indian Agent

Hon. Thomas Murphy,
Superintendent Indian Affairs.

APPENDIX G

BATTLE OF THE ARICKAREE

Dismal failure of the Hancock expedition convinced army chiefs that the soldiers would have to fight the Indians after their own fashion to achieve any measure of success. Among those eager to take the lead was Major George A. Forsyth of General Sheridan's staff. He asked and received permission to recruit a company of frontiersmen acquainted with Indians and the Indian's mode of fighting.

Forsyth was not long recruiting the fifty-one men authorized. They were armed with the very latest in rifles, Spencer repeaters with a capacity for seven cartridges and with Colt's revolvers.

These scouts, with Lieutenant Fred Beecher, second in command, took the field late in August, moving out of Fort Hays in search of any Indians who might be encountered. For nearly two weeks they searched in vain. Then they struck the trail of a small band, which finally entered the broad trail of a large party. It was the trail of Pawnee Killer's Sioux whom Custer and Hancock had contacted the previous year, and a few Cheyennes and Arapahoes. Among the Cheyenne notables in this party were Tall Bull, White Horse and Roman Nose.

During the afternoon of September 16, Forsyth lost trace of the Indians and went into camp on the banks of the Arickaree fork of the Republican River. That night Indians attempted to stampede his horses. At daybreak a large force of Indians was discovered about to attack. The scouts took refuge on a small island covered by tall grasses and a few cottonwood saplings. They shot their horses and covered them with sand to form crude breastworks.

As the whooping line neared the troops, it divided, part going to the right, part to the left of the island. The Indians discharged their rifles at the soldiers, some of whom still were outside their improvised fortress. Forsyth and Beecher were both wounded during this opening fusillade, the commander-in-chief through the legs and Beecher mortally.

Out of range, the Indians reversed their charge and swept back past the little group, now all behind their ramparts. Then the attack became disorganized, the warriors milling around and firing from all sides.

Unable to dislodge their enemies, the Indians began fighting on foot, creeping up close to the breastworks and shooting every time a soldier exposed his head.

Belated arrival of Roman Nose again sent the besiegers to horse. They followed Roman Nose in a headlong dash toward the island. Scarcely had the charging avalanche cleared the bank than Roman Nose toppled from his horse, shot through the back. Hidden in the tall grass of the river's bank were Jack Stilwell and a companion who had detached themselves from the island group and had been firing from their sniping post. Roman Nose died before sundown. Stilwell's bullet had slain the greatest warrior on the Southern Plains, even though that warrior never had been honored by the title of chief.

By sundown, too, several of the soldiers had been killed, including Lieutenant Beecher, and others had been seriously wounded.

Next day the soldiers discovered they were in for a siege, the Indians being more cautious in their attack, confident that they had the scouts at their mercy. That night Stilwell and a companion, Trodeau, slipped through the cordon of Indians and headed for Fort Wallace, more than one hundred miles distant, to bring help.

Followed nearly a week of anxiety and intense suffering. Water was scarce. Rations had become exhausted and the horse flesh upon which they had been subsisting became putried. Nearly half the party were nursing wounds, most of which had become infected. Then came rescue. Stilwell and Trodeau had met a scouting party from Fort Wallace. These soldiers spared neither horse nor rider in returning to the scene of battle. At their approach, the Indians fled.

APPENDIX

Lieutenant Beecher, Dr. J. H. Mooers, the surgeon, and six others were dead. The Indians lost less than a dozen warriors, Roman Nose, Dry Throat, White Weasel Bear, White Thunder, Prairie Bear, Little Man and Killed-by-a-Bear.

APPENDIX H

Among those who held the Indians entirely to blame for the situation in Western Kansas was Governor Samuel J. Crawford, of Kansas who sent the following message to the President:

TOPEKA, KANSAS, AUGUST 17, 1868.

To His Excellency, Andrew Johnson, President:

I have just returned from Northwest Kansas, the scene of a terrible Indian massacre. On the thirteenth and fourteenth, inst., forty of our citizens were killed and wounded by the hostile Indians. Men women and children were murdered indiscriminately. Many of them were scalped and their bodies mutilated. Women, after receiving mortal wounds, were outraged and otherwise inhumanly treated in the presence of their dying husbands and children. Two young ladies and two little girls were carried away by the red-handed assassins to suffer a fate worse than death. Houses were robbed and burned and a large quantity of stock driven off.

The settlers, covering a space sixty miles wide, and reaching from the Saline to the Republican, were driven in, the country laid in ashes and the soil drenched in blood. How long must we submit to such atrocities? Need we look to the Government for protection or must the people of Kansas protect themselves? If the Government cannot control these uncivilized barbarians, while they are under its fostering care and protection, it certainly can put a stop to the unbearable policy of supplying them with arms and ammunition, especially while they are waging war notoriously against frontier settlements, from the borders of Texas to the plains of Dakota. The savage devils have become intolerable and must and shall be driven out of this state. General Sheridan is doing and has done, all in his power to protect our people, but he is powerless for want of troops. If volunteers are needed, I will, if desired, furnish the Government all that may be necessary to insure a permanent and lasting peace.

S. J. CRAWFORD, Governor of Kansas.

President Johnson referred this matter to the War Department and on October 9, 1868, Governor Crawford received the following telegram:

HEADQUARTERS DEPARTMENT OF THE MISSOURI, IN THE FIELD, FORT HAYS, Oct. 9th, 1868.

His Excellency, S. J. Crawford, Governor of Kansas:

Under directions received through Lieutenant General W. T. Sherman, commanding Military Division of the Missouri, from the Hon. Secretary of War, I am authorized to call on you for one regiment of mounted volunteers to serve for a period of six months, unless sooner discharged, against the hostile Indians of the plains. I therefore request that you furnish said regiment as speedily as possible to be rendezvoused and mustered into service of the United States at Topeka, Kansas.

The regiment to consist of one colonel, three majors, twelve captains, twelve first lieutenants, twelve second lieutenants, twelve companies of one hundred men each, including the required number of non-commissioned officers specified in the U. S. Army regulations (1868) the pay, allowances and emoluments of officers and men to be the same as that of U. S. troops.

The men will be rationed from the time of their arrival at the rendezvous and will be furnished with arms, equipment, horses and clothing from the date of muster into the service of the U. S.

I have the honor to be, very respectfully,

Your obedient servant,

P. H. SHERIDAN, Maj. Gen., U. S. A.

Twenty days later the full regiment of twelve hundred men had been assembled at Camp Crawford, half a mile below Topeka, and were being fully equipped for service during a winter campaign.

Governor Crawford resigned as chief executive of the State of Kansas to command the regiment as its colonel. Horace L. Moore was commissioned lieutenant colonel. Commander of Company H was David L. Payne, later to become famous by attempting to colonize portions of the Indian country, before Congress had opened this region to settlement.

APPENDIX I

Most of the popular versions of the Battle of the Washita have been written from Custer's own account, as related in his "Life on the Plains."

Various other writers have quoted other soldier participants, their stories in every instance being so replete with egotism and incongruities as to give grounds for serious questiion of their accuracy. None ever was able to account for the manner in which Major Elliott's detachment became separated from Custer's main command or the details of his last stand. One such dramatic, imaginative account, published by an army officer who boasted thirty-three years' service among the Plains Indians is so typical as to warrant reproduction in part, here for the purpose of illustrating the untrustworthiness of such accounts.

He wrote:

"Wounded in several places, his ammunition expended, Sergeant Major Kennedy stood alone, sabre in hand, surrounded by the crowd of exultant savages. Not a shot was fired at him. No effort was made to kill him, but several Indians approached him with hands stretched out, "How, How."

"Too well he knew the meaning of this kindly demonstration. Merciful death had overtaken all his gallant comrades. He was to be reserved for all the horrors of torture. In his prolonged agonies were his enemies to find consolation for the injuries the troops had inflicted upon them.

"Realizing all, he saw that his only hope of escaping torture was in so exasperating the Indians that they would kill him at once. Seeming to surrender, he advanced toward the chief. They approached each other, hands extended. Quick as thought, Kennedy's sword passed through the chief's body. One instant of terrified surprise on the part of the Indians; the next, twenty bullet holes in Kennedy's body."

The reader is urged to contrast this version with that contained in this chapter and draw his own conclusions.

Again, in the archives of the adjutant general's office at Oklahoma City is a letter to J. B. Thoburn, then curator of the Oklahoma Historical Society, written by Colonel Albert Barnitz, one of the two officers of Custer's command, wounded in the actual fighting in the immediate vicinity of Black Kettle's village. Colonel Barnitz was writing in answer to Mr. Thoburn's request for an account of how the colonel obtained his wound—a bullet in the body.

Colonel Barnitz wrote:

"I did not charge through or into the village, but, all alone, on the upland about three-quarters of a mile from the sandhills, I rode alone and unattended into a crowd of about four hundred warriors running for their ponies. I engaged in a duel with a solitary warrior armed with a gun, one of the Lancaster muzzle-loading guns, with octagonal barrel and brass-lidded patch box in the stock, carrying a big round bullet."

To begin with, there were not more than 300 Indians in Black Kettle's village, including women and children; probably not more than seventy-five warriors all told. These were not gathered in crowds but had scattered in every direction as soon as they discovered the village was being attacked.

It is apparent from a letter written by Custer to his wife, immediately after the battle, that Barnitz, at the time he was carried in from where he had been shot, had indicated his assailants were only two and that he had killed both of them. Custer wrote:

"Colonel Barnitz was wounded by a rifle ball through his bowels. We all regarded him as mortally wounded at first, but he is almost certain to recover now. He acted very gallantly, killing two Indians before receiving his wound."

The reader is asked to compare these accounts, contradictory within themselves, with the straightforward, feasible recital of Magpie's experiences included in this chapter.

When Magpie reached the point in his story where he told of shooting a soldier off his horse, the author sensed he was obtaining the true story of the wounding of Colonel Barnitz, at last. The spot where Magpie said he and his companion were charged by a single horseman was the identical location where both Custer and Barnitz said the Colonel had met disaster. Asked to describe the soldier he had shot, Magpie said he was a big man, some kind of a "chief," because he had some kind of insignia on his uniform. He said he was riding a big brown horse.

Barnitz was an unusually large man and he was riding a brown horse at the time.

In order to obtain the true story of the actual Battle of the Washita, the writer visited the battlefield on more than one occasion, accompanied by Magpie, Little Beaver and Left Hand, three survivors of that massacre. These old Indians were taken to the battlefield that they might have the advantage of being on the very ground where the fight, or massacre, took place, to aid them in reconstructing an accurate recital of incidents which happened that eventful November 27, 1868.

These three were selected from a score or more survivors, because each of them had personal knowledge of the movements of Elliott's men. As a result of this fortunate circumstance, the mystery of how Elliott's detachment came to be separated from Custer's main command and annihilated has been solved completely. In many of the salient points it is substantiated by the account given George Bird Grinnell by other Indians several years previously and related in his "Fighting Cheyennes," page 291.

Barnitz's letters, previously referred to, account for Elliott's movements from the time he left Custer, shortly after midnight, until the massacre started. Magpie accounts for them from shortly thereafter until Elliott's squad captured the little band of women and children, which included Little Beaver.

Little Beaver was an eye-witness to everything that transpired up to the time of the killing of Sergeant-Major Kennedy. He then was taken up behind an Arapahoe and carried to the Arapahoe village of Little Raven. During this ride, he saw Elliott's men overtake Blind Bear and Hawk and shoot them down.

Left Hand was one of the nine Arapahoes who

cut off Elliott's retreat and delayed his progress until he was completely surrounded. He then participated in the siege of Elliott's men and was one of the first to follow Tobacco in the cleanup charge. He even was able to name the four Arapahoes who killed Kennedy.

The writer went over the entire fight with them several times, extracting all possible information, and believes this is the first and only time the complete story of what happened to Kennedy's detachment ever has been written.

APPENDIX J

Elliott's ill-fated chase of Blink Bear and Hawk had an interesting modern sequel. In the summer of 1930, while Magpie and Little Beaver were on the old battlefield, reconstructing the story of that engagement, for this narrative, Little Beaver pointed out to our party the spot where he saw Elliott's men overtake and shoot down these youthful Cheyenne martyrs. He said Blink Bear's relatives came back the next day and carried his body away for burial. Hawk was buried in a shallow grave near where he had fallen.

In the party listening to this recital was Judson Cunningham, court clerk of Roger Mills County, Oklahoma, of which Cheyenne is the county seat. Cunningham long had been interested in this historic engagement and had, from time to time, searched the area for relics of the fight. He recalled that many years before, while a cut for a railroad was being made through the hill where Hawk had been buried, the workmen had unearthed a skeleton of an Indian. These bones had been collected in a box and still were in the possession of John Cassady, editor of the Cheyenne Star. After a careful examination of these relics and the place where they had been found, the old Indian expressed the firm belief that they were the remains of that Indian hero. Magpie expressed the desire that they be recommitted to earth.

It was agreed that, on the next anniversary of the Washita massacre, then only a few weeks in the future, this should be done. At the same time a movement would be launched to have the battlefield declared a national monument and Congress would be asked to erect a suitable monument thereon.

November 27, 1930, sixty-two years after the battle, this burial took place. The largest assemblage in the history of Roger Mills County gathered for the occasion. With full military honors, accorded them by the Cheyenne post of the American Legion, what had been identified as the remains of Hawk were buried on an elevation just south of the bend in which Black Kettle's village had been located. A modest monument has been erected there and Congress will be asked to develop the ancient battlefield as a national monument, similar to that on the Little Big Horn, where Custer met the same fate he had meted to the Indians of Black Kettle's village eight years previously.

APPENDIX K

Following is General Sheridan's official report of the Battle of the Washita, evidently penned upon receipt of Custer's own report to his superior sent ahead of the returning column by courier. It is dated November 29, 1868, the second day following the engagement on the Washita. Custer's column did not reach Camp Supply until December 2.

HEADQUARTERS DEPARTMENT OF THE MISSOURI, IN THE FIELD, DEPOT ON THE NORTH CANADIAN, AT THE JUNCTION OF BEAVER CREEK, INDIAN TERRITORY, November 29, 1868.

GENERAL FIELD ORDERS NO. 6—The Major General commanding announces to this command the defeat, by the Seventh regiment of cavalry, of a large force of Cheyenne Indians, under the celebrated chief Black Kettle, reenforced by the Arapahoes under Little Raven, and the Kiowas under Satanta, on the morning of the 27th instant, on the Washita river, near the Antelope Hills, Indian Territory, resulting in a loss to the savages of one hundred three warriors killed, including Black Kettle, the capture of fifty-three squaws and children, eight hundred and seventy-five ponies, eleven hundred and twenty-three buffalo robes and skins, five hundred and thirty-five pounds of powder, one thousand and fifty pounds of lead, four thousand arrows, seven hundred pounds of tobacco, besides rifles, pistols, saddles, bows, lariats, and immense quantities of dried meat and other winter provisions, the complete destruction of their village, and almost total annihilation of this Indian band.

The loss to the Seventh Cavalry was two officers killed, Major Joel H. Elliott and Captain Louis McL. Hamilton and nineteen enlisted men; three officers wounded, Brevet Lieutenant-Colonel Albert Barnitz (badly), Bretvet Lieutenant-Colonel T. W. Custer, and Second Lieutenant T. Z. March (slightly), and eleven enlisted men.

The energy and rapidity shown during one of the heaviest snow-storms that has visited this section of the country, with the temperature below freezing point, and the gallantry and bravery displayed, resulting in such signal success, reflect the highest credit upon both the officers and men of the Seventh

Cavalry; and the Major General commanding, while regretting the loss of such gallant officers as Major Elliott and Captain Hamilton, who fell while gallantly leading their men, desires to express his thanks to the officers and men engaged in the battle of the Washita, and his special congratulations are tendered to their distinguished commander, Brevet Major General George A. Custer, for the efficient and gallant services rendered, which have characterized the opening of the campaign against hostile Indians south of the Arkansas.

By command of
MAJOR GENERAL P. H. SHERIDAN.
(Signed) J. SCHUYLER CROSBY, Brevet Lieutenant
Colonel, A. D. C., A. A. A. General.

And here is a portion of Custer's own report, from which the above apparently was taken, as quoted on page 39 of Mrs. Custer's "Following the Guidon:"

HEADQUARTERS SEVENTH CAVALRY,
CAMP ON WASHITA, November 28, '68

On the morning of the 26th, eleven companies of the Seventh Calary struck an Indian trail numbering one hundred (not quite twenty-four hours old) near the point where the Texas boundary line crosses the Canadian River.

When the Osage trailers reported a village within a mile of the advance, the column was countermarched and withdrawn to a retired spot to avoid discovery. After all the officers had reconnoitered the location of the village, which was situated in a strip of heavy timber, the command was divided into four columns of nearly equal strength. One was to attack in the woods from below the village. The second was to move down the Washita and attack from the timber from above. The third was to attack from the crest north of the village, while the fourth was to charge from the crest overlooking the village on the left bank of the Washita. The columns were to charge simultaneously at dawn of day; though some of them had to march several miles to gain their positions, three of them made the attack so near together that it seemed like one charge. The fourth was only a few minutes late. The men charged and reached the lodges before the Indians were aware of their presence. The moment the advance was ordered the band struck up "Garryowen," and with cheers every trooper, led by his officer, rushed toward the village. The warriors rushed from their lodges and posted themselves behind trees and in deep ravines, from which they began a most determined resistance. Within ten minutes after the charge the lodges and all their contents were in our possession, but the real

— 310 —

fighting, such as has been rarely, if ever, equalled in Indian warfare, began when attempting to drive out or kill the warriors posted in ravines or ambush. Charge after charge was made, and most gallantly, too, but the Indians had resolved to sell their lives as dearly as possible. The conflict ended after some hours. The entire village, numbering (47) forty-seven lodges of Black Kettle's band of Cheyennes, (2) two lodges of Arapahoes, (2) two lodges of Sioux—(51) fifty-one lodges in all, under command of their principal chief, Black Kettle—were conquered.

The Indians left on the ground (103) one hundred and three warriors, including Black Kettle, whose scalp was taken by an Osage guide. 875 horses and mules were captured, 241 saddles (some of fine and costly workmanship), 573 buffalo robes, 390 buffalo skins for lodges, 160 untanned robes, 210 axes, 140 hatchets, 35 revolvers, 47 rifles, 535 pounds of powder, 1050 pounds of lead, 4,000 arrows and arrowheads, 75 spears, 90 bullet moulds, 35 bows and quivers, 12 shields, 3300 pounds of bullets, 775 lariats, 940 buckskin saddlebags, 470 blankets, 93 coats, 700 pounds of tobacco; all the winter supply of dried buffalo meat, all the meal, flour, and other provisions; in fact, all they possessed was captured, as the warriors escaped with little or no clothing. Everything of value was destroyed. Fifty-three prisoners were taken, squaws and children; among the prisoners are the survivors of Black Kettle and the family of Little Rock. Two white children, captives of the Indians, were captured. A white boy, 10 years old, a captive, had his entrails ripped out with a knife by a squaw. The Kiowas, under Satanta, and Arapahoes, under Little Raven, were encamped six miles below Black Kettle's village. The warriors from these two villages came to attempt rescue of the Cheyennes. They attacked the command from all sides, about noon, hoping to recover the squaws and the herd of the Cheyennes.

Though displaying great boldness, about three o'clock the cavalry counter-charged, and they were driven in all directions and pursued several miles. The entire command was then moved in search of the villages of the Kiowas and Arapahoes, but after an eight-mile march it was ascertained that they had taken fright at the fate of the Cheyennes and fled.

The command was then three days' march from the train of supplies, and the trail having led over a country cut up by ravines and other obstructions, difficult even for cavalry, it was impossible to bring the wagons on. The supplies which each man carried were nearly exhausted, the men were wearied from loss of sleep, and the horses in the same condition for want of forage. About 8 p. m. the return march was begun, and continued until the wagons were reached. In the excitement of the fight, as well as in self-defense, some of the squaws and a few children were killed and wounded; the latter were brought on under medical care. Many of the squaws were taken with arms in their hands, and several soldiers were wounded by them. In one small ravine 38 warriors were found dead, showing the desperation of the conflict. Two officers, Major Elliott and Captain Hamilton, were killed, and 19 enlisted men. Captain Barnitz was seriously wounded.

Many of the statements contained in the above, particularly in regard to the number of Indian warriors killed and the distance down-stream the column progressed before counter-marching, have been disputed by white scouts who accompanied Custer and by the Indians, themselves.

APPENDIX L

The following letters, true copies of the originals now reposing in the National Archives in Washington, D. C., controvert many of the assertions contained in the official reports of General Custer, General Sheridan and General Sherman relative to the Battle of the Washita.

J. S. Morrison was one of Custer's scouts during the Washita Campaign, but evidently went north to Fort Dodge immediately after Custer returned to Camp Supply from his first invasion of the Washita country and did not accompany the second expedition.

E. W. Wynkoop, was agent for the Kiowas and Comanches, but resigned from the Indian Service immediately after the Washita Campaign.

(Letter of J. S. Morrison, one of the Sheridan-Custer scouts, written to E. W. Wynkoop, Indian Agent.)

FORT DODGE, KANS.,
Dec. 14th, 1868.

Dear Col:

I arrived at this place yesterday all right. J. L. Bey accompanied me. He has recovered entirely from the slight indisposition he was laboring under when you left him in Topeka. He has obtained a situation under Major Inman who has got in today from the south.

John Smith, John Poysell and Jack Fitzpatrick have got in today. John S. was not in the fight (Battle of the Washita) but John P. and Jack were. They all agree in stating that the official reports of the fight were very much exaggerated that there was not over twenty Bucks killed, the rest, about forty, were women and children. The prisoners have got in today. They consisted of 53 women and children. One boy is an Arapahoe. The rest are all Cheyennes. Mrs. Crocker is amongst them. She is badly wounded. She says that her child is killed. (Custer reported the child and Mrs. Crocker both killed by the Indians when the fight started, but apparently the truth of the matter is that both were struck by soldier bullets, instead of being the victims of the Indians, else the Indians would have been certain of killing, instead of merely wounding, the mother.—Author) The women say that Black Kettle is killed.

The prisoners will be taken to Fort Riley. It is possible that I will be sent in charge of them. Genls. Sheridan and Custer have started on a new expedition. The officers say that he is going direct to Fort Cobb, swearing vengeance on INDIANS AND INDIAN AGENTS INDISCRIMINATELY. When John's wife (a Cheyenne) heard of the fight she tried to kill herself, first with a knife and next with strychnine but Dr. Howard cured her from the effects of it. John starts for Larned tonight.

John S. Sends his respects to you and requests that you will attend to the business that he entrusted to you or if it is impossible for you to do so that you will turn over the power of attorney to Gen. Sanborn to attend to it for him.

Gers is here and sends his respects to you. He got into trouble and will (be) ordered away from Fort Larned. He is in his old business here.

If you return again to Indian affairs, please to let me know if you can do anything for me. I should like very much to be with you again. There is no difficulty in obtaining employment here. I have half a dozen offers and do not know which to accept but would leave everything to be with you. The Courier is about to start, so

Godbye until we meet again which will be some time.

Very Respect,

J. S. MORRISON

(National Archives, Indian Bureau Records, No. 32)

PHILADELPHIA, PA., JANUARY 26, 1869.

Hon. N. G. Taylor,
Commissioner of Indian Affairs:

Sir:—

In reply to your request to be furnished with all the information I have received relative to the "Battle of the Washita;" I have the honor to state that all the information I have in regard to that affair has been gleaned from the public reports of the same, and in two letters I have received from Mr. James S. Morrison, who was formerly in the employ of my Agency. One of his letters I herewith enclose, the other is in the possession of Col. S. F. Topper, of the Indian Peace Commission. I am perfectly satisfied that the position of "Black Kettle" and his immediate relatives at the time of the attack upon their village was not a hostile one.

I know that "Black Kettle" had proceeded to a point at which he was killed with the understanding that it was the locality where all those Indians who were friendly disposed should assemble. I know that such information had been conveyed to "Black Kettle" as the orders of the military authorities, and that he was also instructed that Fort Cobb was the point that the friendly Indians would receive subsistance at and it is admitted by General Hazen who is stationed at Fort Cobb, that "Black Kettle" had been at his headquarters a few days previous to his death: In regard to the charge that "Black Kettle" engaged in the depredations committed on the Saline river during the summer of 1868. I know that same to be utterly false as "Black Kettle" at the time was camped near my Agency on the Pawnee Fork; the said depredations were undoubtedly committed by a party of Cheyenne Indians, but the same party proceeded with the Sioux north from that point, and up to the time of "Black Kettle's" death had not returned to the Arkansas river. There have been Indians deserving of punishment but unfortunately they have not been those who received at the hands of the troops at the "Battle of the Washita" "Black Kettle's" village at the time of the attack upon it was situated upwards of one hundred and fifty miles from any traveled road in the heart of the Indian Country, and the military reports state that the ground was covered with snow and the weather intensely cold; it is well known that the major portion of the village consisted of women and children and yet the **military reports** are that they were engaged in hostilities and excuse the attack for the reason that evidence was found in the camp, that the said Indians were engaged in hostilities.—How did they know that those evidences existed previous to the assault? Mr. Morrison states that there were 50 (?40) women and **children** killed, that fact need no comment, it speaks for itself. I do not know whether the Government desires to look at this affair in a humane light or not, and if it only desires to know whether it was **right** or **wrong** and disgraceful. With much respect,

Your Obedient Servant,

E. W. WYNKOOP, late U. S. Indian Agent.

CONQUEST OF THE SOUTHERN PLAINS

(National Archives, Indian Bureau Records, No. 2178)

OFFICE SUPERINTENDENT INDIAN AFFAIRS,
ATKINSON, KANSAS, DECEMBER 4, 1868.

Sir:

I have the honor to report that on my return yesterday from Paola, whither I had been to pay the fall annuities to Indians of the Osage River Agency, I found in the public journals, General Sheridan's report of what he calls "the opening of the campaign against the hostile Indians", the perusal of which made me sick at heart. Had these Indians been hostile, or had they been the warriors who committed the outrages upon the white settlers on the Solomon and Saline rivers in August last, or those who subsequently fought Col. Forsyth and his scouts, no one would rejoice over the victory more than myself. But who were the parties thus attacked and slaughtered by General Custer and his command? It was Black Kettle's band of Cheyennes. Black Kettle, one of the best and truest friends the whites have ever had, amongst the Indians of the Plains, he who in 1864, purchased with his own ponies the white women and children captured on the Blue and Platte rivers by the Dog Soldiers of the Cheyenne and by the Sioux, and freely delivered them up at Denver City to Col. Chivington, who was at the time the military commandant at that place. After this he was induced, under promises of protection for his people, to bring them into the vicinity of Fort Lyons, where they were soon afterwards pounced upon by the military led by Chivington and cruelly and indiscriminately murdered. Black Kettle escaped—but his people, in consequence of the step he had taken to induce them to come to the vicinity of the Fort refused to recognize him as their Chief, and he thus remained in disfavor with them up to the time of the treaty of 1865, at which time, after explanations on the part of the Commissioners he was reinstated. In July, 1867, when Gen. Hancock burned the villages of peaceful Cheyennes and Sioux, Black Kettle used all his influence to prevent the Cheyennes from going to war to avenge this wrong, and so persistent were his efforts in this behalf, that his life was threatened, and he had to steal away from them in the night with his family and friends and flee to safety to the lodges of the Arapahoes.

In August, 1867, when I was sent out by the Indian Peace Commission with instructions to assemble in the vicinity of Fort Larned, all the friendly Indians belonging to the Kiowas, Comanches, Arapahoes, Cheyennes and Apaches with a view of using them to get into communication with the hostile

Indians. Black Kettle was among the first to met me at Fort Larned cheerfully proffered me his assistance and protection, and from that day to the conclusion of the treaty of Medicine Lodge Creek, no man worked more assiduously than did he to bring to a successful termination the business then in hand and no man, red or white, felt more happy than did he when his people had finally signed the treaty by which they once more placed themselves upon friendly relations with the Government, and when he ascertained that some of the young men of his tribe had committed the atrocities upon the Solomon and Saline in August last, I have been credibly informed that so great was his grief, he tore his hair and his clothes. And naturally supposing that the whites would wreak vengeance upon all Indians that might chance to fall in their way, and remembering the treachery that had once well nigh cost his life. (I refer to the massacre at Sand Creek) he went south to avoid the impending troubles.

This same report says the family of Little Raven of the Arapahoes is among the prisoners and that he too was engaged in the fight. When I recollect that this Chief was one of those who met me at Fort Larned in September, 1867, furnished me with a guard of his young men from that post to Medicine Lodge Creek, protected me and the few white men with me while there, vigilantly watching over us both day and night continually sending out his warriors as messengers to the hostile Indians for the purpose of inducing them to abandon the path and to come in and meet the Commissioners and finally believing that Little Raven has not been engaged in the recent depredations nor would have permitted any of his warriors to go upon the warpath could he have prevented it. I cannot but feel that the innocent parties have been made to suffer for the crimes of others.

It is likewise said in the report that Sa-tan-ta came to the assistance of Black Kettle. I regret that he has been drawn into these difficulties. He is one of the most powerful chiefs among the Kiowas, and his influence for the last three years has been exerted in favor of peace. Had it not been for him in August last, a desperate fight might have taken place at Fort Zarah between the Kiowas and the soldiers of that post. (See my letter, 22" August last enclosing one from Agent Wynkoop reporting the affair.)

Knowing these Chiefs as I do, I feel satisfied that when all the facts pertaining to the late attack, shall become know it will be found that they and the few lodges with them composed that portion of their tribe who desired to remain at peace, and who were endeavoring to make their way to Fort Cobb for the purpose of placing themselves under the care of their Agents on their new reservation.

Judging from the map of the Indian country this fight took place within some sixty or seventy miles of the latter post, and being so near it confirms the fears I entertained as expressed in my letter to you on the 15th. ult. and will have the effect I apprehend of frightening away all those Indians who were expected to congregate in the vicinity of Fort Cobb, and of starting upon the war path many Indians who have been friendly disposed towards the Government, thus costing the Nation many valuable lives and millions of treasure.

Had Congress at its last session appropriated sufficient funds to continue the feeding of these Indians last June, I believe we could have kept them at peace, and that by this time they would have been quietly located on their new reservation, where we could control and manage them, gradually wean them from their wild and wandering life and in doing which it would not have cost the Government as much per year as it is now costing per month to fight them, and this cause would have been far more humane and becoming a magnanimous and Christian nation.

Very respectfully, your obedient servant,

THOMAS MURPHY, Supt. Indian Affairs.

Hon N. G. Taylor,
Commissioner, Washington, D. C.

DARLINGTON, THE METROPOLIS OF OKLAHOMA TERRITORY

APPENDIX M

SPEECHES OF LITTLE RAVEN AND STONE CALF, TREMONT TEMPLE, BOSTON, 1871—REPORT OF COMMISSIONER OF INDIAN AFFAIRS, 1871, Page 35.

(Little Raven)

My friends, these big chiefs on the left and right have invited me into this big council house and invited us to hear what you have got to say. This is a good house; just the kind of a house to have a good talk in.

Some years ago General Sheridan (and Custer) met my tribe in the Wichita Mountains and told us that he did not want the Arapahoes to fight any more. It was a good talk and I listened to what the General told me.

I have kept the talk ever since and have not fought with the white man.

I want you to look upon these (Indian) men around me. They do not look so strong as they really are; but they are not to be despised, even if they are Indians.

My people, the Arapahoes, the braves and the women and all are anxiously looking for my return. They want to know what kind of talk the White Father made for us. My friends are waiting for me; they are now looking for me and I am glad I have got so good a talk to carry back to them, as I have received here. When I sleep at night I sleep with all this talk in my heart, and when I wake up I find it still there. I am going to take very word of it home with me.

Once the Arapahoes had a fine home in the West but the white man has driven us from there. I hope some day the white man will do justice to the Arapahoes.

There are a great many chiefs listening to what I say tonight and I want to say that I only ask justice for the Arapahoes. I am growing old and

I may die, but my children will live and I hope justice will be done my children if not to myself.

The Great Spirit gave this country to the Indian and the Great Spirit sent the white man here; but I don't think the Great Spirit sent the white man to do injustice to the Indian always. When I get home I shall talk to my young men, to any of them that are disposed to do wrong, and tell them to hold on and to behave themselves.

I think my white brethren I have seen here have made a great talk and that they mean what they say.

(Stone Calf)

Friends, I have recently received an invitation from the President, our Great Father in Washington. This gentleman, the Indian Agent, went from his own country to where we live with our invitation and we at once accepted it and we at once started for the East to see our Great Father in Washington. On our arrival there we found that he was kind to us but we did not have much to say to him.

Our Friend, Little Raven—he is our friend; we are of two different nations, but we live like one nation—inasmuch as Little Raven, our great friend, has spoken to you and told you the wishes and thoughts of his tribe, you may consider it as much for the Cheyennes as for the Arapahoes.

Only a remnant of our once powerful tribe is left. A few years ago they were in trouble with the Government, not from any cause that we created ourselves, but from abuses of western white men who are on the borders and constantly clashing with us.

We have made several treaties with the United States Government. In this last treaty of 1867 there were seven commissioners sent out to talk with us in regard to living in peace with the American people. But their promises made then have never been fulfilled; they have never been complied with, while ours have been.

Now, why are we confined to this small strip of country that is left us in return for the whole territory that belonged to us?

They said they would teach our people to plant and raise corn, and to build our lodges from trees.

But before they ever plowed or planted an acre of corn for us they commenced to build railroads through our country. What use have we for railroads in our country? What have we to transport from our nation? Nothing. We are living wild, really living on the prairies as we have lived in former times. I do not see that we have been benefitted in the least by all the treaties that we have made with the United States Government. We wish the Government, at present, with the aid of this association here, to stop the railroads from going through our country until we have some way to support ourselves there. We haven't an ox. We have not an acre of corn growing today in our great country that the Government has said they would reserve for us.

I speak of railroads, not that we have any objections to railroads if we had any use for them; but you can't build railroads through our territory without white men being left among us on each side of the railroad and they will come in conflict with us. They cannot remain there in peace with the Indian. Bad men are sent to build railroads, and bad men are left among us. We have young men that are foolish. I, for my part, am at peace with the white man and desire to remain at peace with him; but if you send bad men among us, not chiefs like those who are here tonight, we cannot remain at peace.

Printed By
Oklahoma Printing Company
Guthrie, Oklahoma